# IN HIS SERVICE:
## EDUCATORS SERVING GOD AND HIS CHILDREN

# IN HIS SERVICE:
## EDUCATORS SERVING GOD AND HIS CHILDREN

### MATT STEPHEN

**Troitsa Books**
*Commack, New York*

| | |
|---|---|
| Editorial Production: | Susan Boriotti |
| Office Manager: | Annette Hellinger |
| Graphics: | Frank Grucci and Jennifer Lucas |
| Information Editor: | Tatiana Shohov |
| Book Production: | Donna Dennis, Patrick Davin, Christine Mathosian and Tammy Sauter |
| Circulation: | Maryanne Schmidt |
| Marketing/Sales: | Cathy DeGregory |

Library of Congress Cataloging-in-Publication Data
Stephen, Matt.
    In His service : educators serving God and his children / by Matt Stephen.
        p.   cm.
    ISBN 1-56072-505-2
    1. Teachers--Prayer-books and devotions--English.  2.Devotional calenders.  I. Title.
BV4596.T43S74           1997                       97-41237
242'.68--dc21                                               CIP

Copyright © 2000 by Matt Stephen
    Troitsa Books, a division of
    Nova Science Publishers, Inc.
    227 Main Street, Suite 100
    Huntington, New York 11743
    Tele. 516-424-6682       Fax 516-424-4666
    e-mail: Novascience@earthlink.net
    e-mail: Novascil@aol.com
    Web Site: http://www.nexusworld.com/nova

All rights reserved. No part of this book may be reproduced, stored in a retrieval system or transmitted in any form or by any means: electronic, electrostatic, magnetic, tape, mechanical photocopying, recording or otherwise without permission from the publishers.

The authors and publisher have taken care in preparation of this book, but make no expressed or implied warranty of any kind and assume no responsibility for any errors or omissions. No liability is assumed for incidental or consequential damages in connection with or arising out of information contained in this book.

This publication is designed to provide accurate and authoritative information with regard to the subject matter covered herein. It is sold with the clear understanding that the publisher is not engaged in rendering legal or any other professional services. If legal or any other expert assistance is required, the services of a competent person should be sought. FROM A DECLARATION OF PARTICIPANTS JOINTLY ADOPTED BY A COMMITTEE OF THE AMERICAN BAR ASSOCIATION AND A COMMITTEE OF PUBLISHERS.

*Printed in the United States of America*

# DEDICATION

*This book is dedicated to God and all of His children who serve His children*

# CONTENTS

| | |
|---|---|
| **DEDICATION** | v |
| **ACKNOWLEDGMENTS** | xi |
| **INTRODUCTION** | xiii |
| **CHAPTER 1    AUGUST** | **1** |
| A Teacher's Prayer | 2 |
| Two Eggs Over-Easy With A Side Order Of Prayer | 3 |
| Guiding Principles | 4 |
| **CHAPTER 2    SEPTEMBER** | **7** |
| A School is a Haven | 8 |
| Service With a Smile | 9 |
| The Lighthouse | 11 |
| Reputation Building | 13 |
| Heart vs. Stuff | 14 |
| Be the First | 15 |
| Team Spirit | 17 |
| Looking Past the Bad to See the Sad | 18 |
| Professional Dress Code | 20 |
| Hugology | 21 |
| **CHAPTER 3    OCTOBER** | **25** |
| A Lesson from Mother Nature | 26 |
| Time for Trifocals | 28 |
| Dignity | 29 |
| Don't Drive Into the Smoke | 31 |
| Parent Conferences | 32 |

| | |
|---|---|
| Hello World | 34 |
| Right Action - Wrong Reason | 35 |
| Pass it On | 37 |
| Coffee, Tea, or Technology? | 38 |

## CHAPTER 4  NOVEMBER  41

| | |
|---|---|
| Surely You Jest | 42 |
| Crying Over Spilt Children | 43 |
| Where is the Gratitude? | 44 |
| In a Child's Shoes | 46 |
| Be Quick to Listen | 47 |
| In the Eyes of the Beholder | 49 |
| Right at the End of Your Nose | 50 |
| Listen to God | 51 |

## CHAPTER 5  DECEMBER  53

| | |
|---|---|
| Here to Serve | 54 |
| Stoplights of Life | 56 |
| Be a Shining Light | 57 |
| The Biggest Picture | 58 |
| Turn Your Creative Juices Loose | 60 |
| The Week Before Christmas Break | 61 |

## CHAPTER 6  JANUARY  65

| | |
|---|---|
| Post-Christmas Vacation Blues | 66 |
| New Year's Resolutions | 67 |
| Shelter in a Storm | 69 |
| The Proper Focus | 70 |
| Laying Lives Aside | 72 |
| Take Time to Play | 73 |
| Career Crisis or Celebration? | 75 |
| Recipe for Service | 76 |

## CHAPTER 7  FEBRUARY  79

| | |
|---|---|
| The Wrong Crowd | 80 |
| Judging and Changing People | 81 |
| Last Place | 82 |
| Indecision | 84 |
| Freedom bound | 85 |

| | |
|---|---|
| Team-Building | 87 |
| Forgiveness | 88 |
| No Middle Ground | 90 |

## CHAPTER 8     MARCH     93

| | |
|---|---|
| Gentleness | 94 |
| Test of Fortitude | 95 |
| When to Let Go | 97 |
| Can We Take It? | 98 |
| How Great Art Thou? | 100 |
| One Good Friday | 101 |
| Truth or Dare | 102 |
| Go With It | 104 |

## CHAPTER 9     APRIL     107

| | |
|---|---|
| Standardized Tests/ Nonstandardized Children | 108 |
| Meditations | 109 |
| Hide and Seek | 111 |
| Let Go and Let God | 112 |
| One Day at a Time | 114 |
| Secretaries' Day | 115 |
| Dump the Mental Garbage | 116 |
| To Be or Not to Be | 118 |
| Life's Adventures | 120 |

## CHAPTER 10     MAY     123

| | |
|---|---|
| Dumber Words Were Never Spoken | 124 |
| Are You Famous? | 125 |
| Silly Smiles | 127 |
| Take a Number Please | 128 |
| Mother's Day | 129 |
| Moving Up | 130 |
| Serve Whole-Heartedly | 131 |
| Your Symphony | 133 |

## CHAPTER 11     JUNE/JULY     135

| | |
|---|---|
| Final Prayer | 136 |

# ACKNOWLEDGMENTS

I thank my wife, Martha, and my two girls, Elizabeth and Rebecca, for supporting me as we rode the "first-time author roller coaster" together.

I also thank several people who have patiently served as mentors over the last twenty years: Dr Charles Patterson, Superintendent of Killeen ISD; Dr. Ann Farris, Deputy Superintendent; Marvin Rainwater, Principal of Ellison High School; and Dale Hughling, Executive Director of Computer Services.

I also thank several of my ministers for their inspirational words: Stephen Ramsdell, Gary Kindley, and John Robbins.

Finally, I thank my parents and parents-in-law Francis and Gwen Stephen and Gene and Imogene Sorley for their unconditional love. They taught me the most important lesson in life – to love God.

# INTRODUCTION

The spirit of service is in trouble in America. The idea of service is not what it once was. Several decades of "me-first" attitudes have played havoc with the concept of service. This is unfortunate because God put us on this Earth to serve one another and to share His love. We educators are in the ideal profession to carry out God's will. We should be deliriously happy with our work, but we are losing the joy that should rightfully be ours as we serve God and His children. It is my hope that this book will help us mentally, emotionally and spiritually survive the difficult times, as well as celebrate and focus on the joys of the teaching profession.

If you already feel this service spirit, celebrate with me and share our ideas with a friend. If your service spirit is waning, this book will help you look to God for needed inspiration. If you have lost the joy of working with children, ask God to speak to you this year. This book will help you to seek needed faith and strength from the Lord as you renew your service spirit. Once a service spirit is revived within you, everyone will benefit: you, your family, your students, their parents, and your colleagues at work.

This book is divided into the months of the school year (August through June). The challenges and joys of each month of the school year are explored and celebrated. Because of the busy schedule you keep as an educator, the format of this book is set up for approximately two readings per week.

Together, let's reflect on the greatest of callings: to serve God and His children. Let's call upon God to help us to renew our service spirits.

As King David once sang:

> *Create in me a clean heart, O God, and renew a steadfast spirit within me.*
>
> Psalm 51:10 (NKJV)

## CHAPTER 1

# AUGUST

August is the month of preparation. We wrap-up Summer vacation and prepare for the new school year. We are busy organizing our rooms, planning the scope and sequence for the year, getting materials together, and preparing for the opening of school. Several heads are better than one when planning for God's children, so utilize one another's strengths as you plan out the instructional activities for the year. Cooperative planning is what makes schools great.

August is also a time of setting goals for our students, our schools and our districts. We get involved in planning campus goals, staff in-service and school activities for the new year. This is also a time to plan goals for our personal growth. Take time to reflect on your career and set some serious goals to attain this year. You must see to your own professional growth. As well-meaning as administrators try to be in helping you grow professionally, only you are aware of your personal needs. Most important, talk to God regarding His will for you this year. His plans are the greatest of all.

We are also meeting new colleagues and new students. We have new relationships to build and previous relationships to maintain and improve. Make it a priority to meet all of the new staff members on you campus. Be sure to offer your help and check up on them several times before school starts.

There is an air of excitement about the beginning of the new year. Unfortunately, along with the excitement comes a little anxiety. A good night's sleep is hard to get. Ask God for some peaceful sleep as you approach opening day.

## A Teacher's Prayer

Dear Father,

**You are** my counsel and my guide
the guardian and protector at my side.
You are my hope - joy and peace you give,
You are my purpose - my reason to live.

**I admit** that sometimes I am too busy to touch,
sometimes I think of myself too much,
sometimes my patience runs too thin,
sometimes my tunnel vision kicks in.

**Thank You** for allowing me to serve Your children well,
for giving me intelligence and a story to tell,
for giving me freedom of choice in what I do,
for the eternity I get to spend with You.

**Please** make my teaching creative and fun,
supply me with endurance to get my job done,
restore my sense of purpose and focus on others,
 grant me patience with my sisters and brothers

Most of all I pray for my students' future.
As Your instrument I will try to assure
that they grow in character strong and true
and accomplish all you plan for them to do.
              Amen

We need to pray for ourselves and our children every day. As Paul told us:

> *Here are my directions: Pray much for others;*
> *plead for God's mercy upon them; give thanks*
> *for all He is going to do for them.*
>
> 1 Timothy 2:1 (TLB)

Dear Father,
Thank You for our ability to make a difference for Your children. Help us to pray daily on their behalf. With Your guidance, we can teach them Your will and raise them for Your glory.

Amen

## TWO EGGS OVER-EASY WITH A SIDE ORDER OF PRAYER

It is important to start everyday right with a good, healthy breakfast. We need the correct nourishment in order to sustain the necessary energy to function at work and to do our best. A good, healthy breakfast enables our bodies to repair themselves and to grow stronger. Starting the day with a good, healthy breakfast makes us a better person physically.

Paul tells us how to grow in the Lord:

> *And now just as you trusted Christ to save you, trust*
> *him, too, for each day's problems; live in vital union*
> *with him. Let your roots grow down into him and draw*
> *up nourishment from him. See that you go on growing*
> *in the Lord, and become strong and vigorous in the truth*
> *you were taught. Let your lives overflow with joy and*
> *thanksgiving for all he has done.*
>
> Colossians 2:6-7 (TLB)

To grow stronger in the Lord, we need to begin each day with prayer. This communication with God gives us the needed spiritual energy to supply us with motivation to serve God and His children to the best of our abilities. Talking with God first thing in the morning helps us to maintain our priorities and provides us with the proper focus for the day. Communing with God repairs our spirits and makes us stronger.

Dear Father,

More important than a good breakfast, we need to start each day with You! Grant us physical strength and peaceful minds. Please help us focus on Your will and Your purpose for us this day.

Amen

## GUIDING PRINCIPLES

Each of us has a moral code that guides our behavior. Sometimes these codes are referred to as "guiding principles." From the time we wake up until we go to bed, our guiding principles direct our every move. As our students watch us, they learn what principles guide our behaviors. They often incorporate our guiding principles (good and bad) into their own personalities. Because we are role models for our students, our choices of guiding principles become even more crucial.

So what guiding principles are considered to be successful for educators? Here is a short-list:

Be consistent
Praise one another
Encourage and support one another
Be open-minded
Be a leader and a follower
Lead by example
Listen
Be reflective and self-evaluative
Learn from one another

Keep your sense of humor
Be dependable
Be spontaneous
Work together
Be friendly
Be professional
Keep a positive attitude
Be dedicated to children
Keep high expectations
Be patient
Go to the source with concerns
Take advantage of available resources
Be confidential
Use tact and diplomatic language
Be trusting
Be willing to account for your actions
Forgive and forget
Be humble
Don't forget to apologize
Keep people informed
Teach mastery, not material
Be willing to go "the extra mile"
Don't forget to take care of your personal life
Be willing to give and accept criticism with a spirit of love
Be empathetic
Be willing to ask questions
Respect one another's differences and opinions, yet strive for unity
Be fair

It is easy to see how these guiding principles can bring success to educators, but this is quite a checklist for every day behavior! Can we possibly follow all of these guiding principles every minute of the day? Without God's help, it doesn't seem likely.

Jesus tells us how effective we are without Him:

> *"Take care to live in me, and let me live in you. For a branch can't produce fruit when severed from the vine. Nor can you be fruitful apart from me."*
>
> John 15:4 (TLB)

We are promised that alone we will not be fruitful. We will not be able to serve God's children well. As we live in the Lord, we are empowered to do more than we think is humanly possible. Through Jesus we can successfully follow these guiding principles each day and provide the best possible role model for His children. Don't forget to call upon the Lord each morning to ask for His guidance, His peace and His strength.

Dear Father,

Through You all things are possible. Only with Your help can we be superhuman and near-perfect models for Your children. Please help us to maintain the highest of personal standards for ourselves.

Amen

CHAPTER 2

# SEPTEMBER

September is the month of new beginnings and new opportunities. We are building new relationships with our students. We should immediately get to know each child for whom we are working. We must involve ourselves in personal conversation with each child whenever possible. Make it a priority to identify special needs of students right away. This may mean seeking help from other personnel to help meet each student's needs.

We are also establishing our reputations as teachers. Our top priority is to establish control. Many educators will tell a new teacher "not to smile until Christmas." Since first impressions are so important, I think this is bad advice. We need to show our students that we care about them on the first day. We cannot build effective relationships with students unless they know that we care about them. God tells us that we are to love and serve one another. How can we do this without smiling?

This month is also our "training and adjustment" month. We are "training" our students to follow our rules and procedures. Proper instruction of rules, procedures and expectations is important to the students' ability to adjust to a new system. A successful adjustment means great potential for academic success.

This time of year is also a reminder of the importance of loyalties and team spirit. We are busy supporting our grade school, junior high, high school, college and professional sports teams. We are fiercely loyal toward our teams and our fellow fans. What a great feeling it is to be part of a team!

September also signifies the beginning of Autumn with all of the sights, sounds and smells that goes with the season. Open House, PTA activities and football games keep us busy with evening activities.

We are also building relationships with our colleagues. We may already know most of our co-workers, but there is always someone we need to get to know a little better. Don't forget to drop in on the new teachers and offer a listening ear. They need your attention.

## A School is a Haven

A School is a Haven for Children Who:

>are rejected; because they find acceptance with open arms
>have no hope; because they hear words of encouragement
>are not loved; because caring relationships are formed
>are verbally abused; because they hear soft gentle words
>are physically abused; because they receive gentle embraces
>are ridiculed; because they hear words that build confidence
>have no joy; because they can feel a spirit of happiness
>are afraid; because they are protected from harm
>are alone; because friends are found
>are hurting; because they find a listening ear
>have given up; because they find a partner to help build their future

School truly is a haven for some of our children. It is a fact that for some children the only place they receive praise or feelings of positive self-worth is at school. How fortunate for us educators, that we are in a position to enrich the lives of our children!

Often we complain because there is plenty of work to do just teaching the students academics. There is not enough time to teach values, social mores, and citizenship. Time is already our enemy.

Where are we supposed to find the time to be mother and father to some of these children? Like it or not, our society has moved to a point where some parents are abdicating their parental responsibilities. So who is left to take over? The public school system. We educators can look at this as a burden or as an opportunity.

David tells us that God is our refuge:

> *The Lord is my rock and my fortress and my deliverer;*
> *My God, my strength, in whom I will trust; My shield*
> *and horn of my salvation, my stronghold.*
>
> Psalm 18: 2 (NKJV)

We are God's children serving God's children. Just as God is our refuge, we serve as a refuge for His children. We are challenged to respond to His children with the same love and protection that He provides for us.

Dear Father,
Thank You for serving as our refuge. We praise You for knowing our every need and providing comfort for us during our times of distress. Help us to know that through our dedication to You, we can daily provide a refuge for each of Your children.

Amen

## SERVICE WITH A SMILE

Do you remember how the service industry once went out of its way to serve others? At a full-service gas station, your car was gassed-up, checked over, and polished before you drove away. If you got out of the car, it was only to pay a visit to a spotless restroom. Grocery stores and pharmacies delivered goods to your house, doctors made house calls, waiters and counter personnel were friendly and talkative, and banks did not charge for conveniences. Everyone smiled and was glad to be of service!

This service spirit is not totally dead today, but it is severely wounded. Often we see no smiles from those in service positions. We experience little personal interaction, selfish attitudes, slow service, poor quality, and little if no follow-up. Many times I, the customer, am the only one who says, "thank you."

Why the changes in service attitude? Our society has changed, thus causing some services to be outdated. We now have high speed technology and communications which allows our society to take a faster pace. We have developed a "me first" attitude which places everyone around us in a distant second place. Our population has exploded and our mobility has dramatically increased. All of these changes make it more likely that there will be fewer personal interactions among people in the future. Thus, today many of us are developing a more "impersonal" service attitude.

Although times are different, Paul's advice about a service attitude is timeless:

> *Work hard and cheerfully at all you do, just as though you were working for the Lord and not merely for your masters.*
> Colossians 3:23 (TLB)

We are serving the Lord when we serve His children. Because we serve the Lord, we serve with gladness!

As educators, we cannot afford to lose the "service with a smile" attitude. We must work toward more positive customer relations with our children and their parents. We can strive for the highest quality output possible and take joy in sharing these experiences with the children. We can personally ensure our children's success and well-being and know that we can make a difference. With a smile, we can guarantee to our customers that we care about them and their futures!

We are given more advice to help our service attitudes:

*Love each other with brotherly affection and take delight in honoring each other.*

Romans 12:10 (TLB)

We should take delight in honoring our customers. We can dedicate ourselves to "delighting" our students, their parents, and our community!

Dear Father,
We know that we are serving You when we serve Your children. We promise to serve You cheerfully as we honor Your children.

Amen

## THE LIGHTHOUSE

The Lighthouse

> She is larger-than-life and awe inspiring
> as she stands firmly on the ground,
> She slings her light out into the darkness
> turning the lost into the found.
>
> Dependable, patient, stalwart and sturdy
> are some words used to express her charm.
> She is a beacon of light guiding ships in the night
> providing direction and protection from harm.
>
> She guides others on their adventures
> some never to return, their futures skillfully erected.
> She never abandons her post, she always remains behind
> with no accolades expected.

It is often a thankless job ..........
Yet, she is ever faithful to her mission of serving others.

Please forgive me for getting deep or profound
like some philosopher or preacher,
but it seems to me that you could drop the word "lighthouse" and insert the word "teacher".

Educators can be compared to a lighthouse. We spend our lives guiding children as they pass through our schools. We reach out to our wandering students. We help them learn what they need to know and then send them off to bigger and better futures. Hopefully because of us they will lead richer, more satisfying lives. We give our best effort and receive very little praise, yet our existence is essential. We are the guiding lights that our children depend upon to lead them. We are the lighthouses that guide our children toward their futures. We are the firm foundation of our society that molds the next generation for our country!

Jesus tells us that we are the lights that guide others to Him:

> *"Don't hide your light! Let it shine for all; let your good deeds glow for all to see, so that they will praise your heavenly Father."*
>
> Matthew 5:15-16 (TLB)

Dear Father,
Thank You for making us lighthouses to guide others to You. Be our firm foundation so that we can weather the storms as we serve Your children.

Amen

## REPUTATION BUILDING

Do you remember the reputations of some of the teachers that you had as you were growing up? Some were reputed to be easy, hard, nice, mean, fun, boring, etc. I remember that I knew a lot about some teachers before I stepped into their rooms for the first time. Funny thing though, sometimes the reputations were accurate and sometimes they weren't.

Educators have a reputation to build beginning with the first day they walk into a school building. I remember my first few weeks as a new teacher at a high school. As a young-looking 24 year old, it was not uncommon for me to be stopped in the hall by other teachers and asked for my hallway pass. I knew that I needed to build a tough, no-nonsense reputation with my students in a hurry or I would lose control. I diligently worked on that reputation for many years. Also, each time I changed jobs or schools I had to start all over again creating my reputation for the students as well as my colleagues. Each time I pursued the creation of a new reputation, I had a particular one in mind - one to fit the situation.

Everything that we do and say on the job is recorded toward creating our reputation. Our words and our deeds away from work are also cataloged and added to our reputation. So the pressure is on 24 hours a day, 7 days a week. What kind of reputation have you built up to this point? What are the children telling others about you? Are you easy or tough? fair or unjust? caring or indifferent? hard-working or lazy? fun or boring? Is this the reputation you set out to earn?

The Bible tells us how to create a good reputation:

> *If you want favor with both God and man, and a reputation for good judgment and common sense, then trust the Lord completely; don't ever trust in yourself. In everything you do, put God first, and He will direct you and crown your efforts with success.*
> 
> Proverbs 3:4-6 (TLB)

We are not to build our reputations alone. If we trust only in ourselves, we will fail. We are to put God first in everything that we do. We are to trust in God to help us each step of the way. Only through Him can we build the reputation that we need to serve His children according to His will.

Dear Father,
We ask for Your guidance as we build our reputations. Help us to earn the reputation of fair, hard-working, compassionate, interesting, and fun to have as a teacher. We need a good reputation in order to best serve Your children.

Amen

## HEART VS. STUFF

Every year we pursue the perfect program or solution to student achievement. I call this the NIFTY pursuit (New Idea For This Year). Sometimes the concepts are new, but usually they are old ideas repackaged under a new name. I have accumulated a long list of NIFTY experiences: cooperative learning, mastery learning, cognitive brain theory, multiple intelligences, learning theories, learning styles, assertive discipline, cooperative discipline, social skills models, interdisciplinary approaches to instruction, curriculum alignment, etc., and the list gets longer every year.

Although new materials and theories are a helpful part of an educator's repertoire, the true difference in a child's learning comes from relationships established between teacher and student. People make the difference in an organization! All of the newest, most expensive and most effective instructional materials and programs in the world will make no difference if there isn't a quality person to implement them. Moreover, the success of these NIFTY ideas are dependent upon the quality of the personal relationship established between teacher and student. So, it is not what you've got, but who you've got that makes the difference!

God has told us that it is not what we have, but who we are that makes the difference:

> *It isn't sacrificial bullocks and goats that I really want from you. No, I do not need your sacrifices of flesh and blood. What I want from you is your true thanks; I want you to trust me in your times of trouble.*
> Psalm 50: 9,13-15 (TLB)

Gods wants our hearts, not our "stuff." So do our children. The best materials and programs are useless if the students are not motivated to learn. We must concentrate on establishing relationships and rapport with our students. They will work harder if they like and respect their teachers. When children realize that they have our hearts, they will in turn dedicate their hearts and minds to us.

Dear Father,
We have given our hearts away to Your children. Help us to show our students that we care for them and want the best for them. We remember also that You want our hearts, not our stuff.
Amen

## BE THE FIRST

A fourth grade teacher was once told by a parent, "You are the first teacher to say something really nice about my child." Think about it. A fourth grade teacher hears from a parent that she is the first teacher to say something really nice about her child. What a tragedy! This child spent four years with four or more professional teachers with little or no positive feedback given to the parents. If no positive comments were made to the parents, one has to wonder if any caring statements were made to the child.

Children are creating their self-images during the first years of their lives. They are determining their self-worth. Their egos are fragile and vulnerable to criticism. They seek validation from the adults that they respect. Our purpose is to see that each child hears what is good about himself. We are here to save this world one child at a time!

Parents are delighted with us when we demonstrate a true caring attitude toward their children. I have found that I can make all sorts of mistakes as long as the parents know that I care about their children. If they don't think I care about their children, I can do nothing right. This attitude is justified. I feel the same way when I am wearing my "parent hat." I will let "unusual" teaching tactics slip by as long as I think the teacher cares about my child.

I believe we are not only here to serve the children and their parents, we are here to delight them. The Bible tells us that there are rewards for our good deeds:

> *So, two good things happen as a result of your gifts -*
> *those in need are helped, and they overflow with thanks*
> *to God.*
>
> 2 Corinthians 9:12 (TLB)

Not only do we help those who are in need, we inspire others to be thankful to God for dedicated, caring educators. God should receive the thanks for the good that we do for the children. Parents will know to credit God for our good works if we let them know that He is in charge of our lives and our actions.

Assume that no one before you has praised your children or complimented them in front of their parents. If other educators have already done this, then the child and the parents have already been rewarded. If you are the first to praise a child, I believe that you will receive a special blessing for this. Please don't let these opportunities get past you.

Dear Father,

Thank You for the opportunity to teach Your children. You are responsible for every good action that we do. We are Your hands here on Earth. Help us to delight Your children and their parents.

Amen

## TEAM SPIRIT

One weekend I decided to leave education to coach softball. Not really, but I was fired-up over what I witnessed at the school district's Wellness Softball Tournament. There was an air of incredible team spirit permeating our school's softball team. All individual players mixed together to create a "synergy" that surpassed all of our expectations and drove us to win first place in a tournament filled with fierce competition. Let me describe for you some of the team dynamics that enabled us to end up on top.

Our team played six games over a thirteen hour period of fun, yet intense, competition. Everyone had a shared focus and sense of purpose. The coaches never had to stop and remind the players why they were there. Everyone was dedicated to the goal of winning first place. There was an air of mutual admiration and respect. All players had different abilities and talents, yet the competition was not within the team, it was a shared competition against the opponents. The players supported one another through the good times and the bad. There was no gossip. Our players were courageous. They made daring moves for the sake of the team, yet they were cautious when the situation called for it. We cheered each other's accomplishments and offered criticism when needed. Our players showed disappointment when they didn't execute their best. Instead of making excuses, they maintained an attitude of determination not to repeat mistakes. Our team demonstrated an unrelenting endurance to accomplish the goal of first place by continuing to give it their all even after twelve hours of play!

When it was all over, we knew we had accomplished our goal. The exhilaration was incredible! My thought afterwards was "It is too bad that we don't experience this all of the time in other areas of our lives. Team competitions are short and intense. We cannot possibly sustain this level of competitive intensity throughout our daily personal and professional lives. However, we can remember these team-spirit experiences and attempt to incorporate them into our daily routines as often as possible. At our schools, we can exhibit this same team-spirit as we lead our children on to their successes.

Paul gives us some specific ideas about team-spirit:

> *If you love someone, you will be loyal to him no matter what the cost. You will always believe in him, always expect the best of him, and always stand your ground in defending him.*
>
> 1 Corinthians 13:7 (TLB)

If we are to work together as a team, we have to be fiercely loyal toward one another. This means putting others ahead of ourselves. Our colleagues and our children come first. Together through team-spirit, we can accomplish more than we dare to dream.

Dear Father,
   So often we try to do everything by ourselves. Please help us to rely more upon You and others around us to accomplish our goals. Help us to keep a team-spirit.

Amen

## LOOKING PAST THE BAD TO SEE THE SAD

All of us have shared the frustration of teaching children who for one reason or another are "discipline problems." Sometimes all efforts to change the students' behaviors fail and the problems get worse each day. These children's behaviors can consume our lives and make us wish we had pursued another profession. I have seen many good teachers leave the profession, not because of the long hours or the short pay, but because of these difficult children. How do we deal with a child who seems to be dedicated to disrupting other people's lives?

Paul tells us the answer:

> *Blessed be the God and Father of our Lord Jesus Christ, the Father of mercies and God of all comfort, who comforts us in all our tribulation, that we may be able to comfort those who are in any trouble, with the comfort with which we ourselves are comforted by God.*
>
> 2 Corinthians 1: 3-4 (NKJV)

We are told to comfort those who are in trouble. In order to be a comforter, we must look past the "bad" in the child and see the "sad." Behind every incorrigible behavior problem is a hurt child. We must find the hurt. Once we find the inner reason for the child's behavior, we can begin to change the outward behavior. But this takes time!

It is easy to punish children for their misbehavior. The easiest and most efficient punishment is to separate them from the rest of the population: detention, suspension, alternative schools and expulsion. This works for the short term, but it does not provide for any long term cure. It takes time and effort to diagnose the reasons behind the misbehavior and to work on a long term cure. We must take the time to teach the children self-discipline and build important relationships with them. This is a slow step-by-step process that must be started by us, the adults, because students will not take the first step!

The very wise King Solomon once said:

> *Train up a child in the way he should go, And when he is old he will not depart from it.*
>
> Proverbs 22:6 (NKJV)

God plainly tells us that we are to comfort those who are in trouble, not send them away. He also tells us to raise children in His way and not to give up. Our love and attention can be the catalyst for true change in our children's lives.

Dear Father,

Help us to love others as You love us. Give us the wisdom to know how to properly guide Your children and the patience to effectively build these vital relationships.

Amen

## PROFESSIONAL DRESS CODE

The professional dress codes at schools often seem to get more attention than they really deserve. We measure skirts, define shorts and jeans, assign degrees of tightness to clothing, and constantly define and redefine "professional fashion." I am not sure whether certain clothing stimulates teachers to perform their duties better or students to learn better. I will leave that debate to my learned colleagues. But I am sure of one thing - God gives us a dress code which is critical to our success.

Paul tells us which part of a dress code is most important:

> *Don't be concerned about the outward beauty that depends on jewelry, or beautiful clothes, or hair arrangement. Be beautiful inside, in your hearts, with the lasting charm of a gentle and quiet spirit which is so precious to God.*
>
> 1 Peter 3:3-4 (TLB)

Imagine the wonderful climates that would exist in our schools if everyone adhered to God's dress code. If everyone wore gentle and quiet spirits, we would no longer need security police, discipline codes, or alternative schools.

Paul also tells us that our dress code must always be changing for the better:

> *Now your attitudes and thoughts must all be constantly changing for the better. Yes, you must be a new and different person, holy and good. Clothe yourself with this new nature.*
>
> Ephesians 4:23 (TLB)

We should never be satisfied that we are complying with God's dress code. We should always be searching ourselves for better attitudes and more godly behavior.

Dear Father,
Thank You for assigning us the ultimate dress code. We will wear our gentle, quiet spirits for Your children.

Amen

## HUGOLOGY

As an educator, I have researched hugology (the study of hugs) for years. Spending countless hours in the field observing and experiencing various kinds of hugs, I found there is much to be learned from them. I have become an expert, and I would like to share this expertise with you.

Hugs can be classified according to meaning. In the area of adult hugging, there are several types of hugs. First there is the "Hello, how are you? I haven't seen you in a long time" hug. This hug usually takes 2-3 seconds and is usually rough and sometimes even of rib-breaking caliber. Second, there is the "I really care about you, but I don't want to start any rumors" hug. This hug is also 2-3 seconds long, but it is much gentler and more intimate. Then there is the "I love you and don't care what others think" hug. This hug ranges in length according to the situation (usually 5 seconds or longer). This type of hug is reserved for special people in our lives.

Children's hugs can also be categorized according to meaning. First there is the "Hi, great to see you, but I've got to hurry" hug. This hug can range from .001 of a second to 2 seconds depending on the urgency. These hugs can often leave bruises or tell-tale marks (and during the flu/colds season when noses are runny, these hugs can lead to expensive cleaning bills). The second kind of hug is the "I'm really glad to know you" hug. This hug usually lasts about 3-5 seconds. I like these hugs because they are sincere. Then, occasionally you get the "I need you, please protect me" hug. This is a very important hug not to ignore. This hug can last for up to several minutes. We have all been there and know these hugs.

I believe that God put us on this world to give these "protective" hugs when they are needed. They pop-up at the strangest times for usual and unusual reasons. Children are much more likely to ask for them than adults, but adults need them just the same. It is easy to recognize a child's need for a protective hug because he/she won't let go! With older students and adults, one needs to be more attune to signals. There is one irrefutable fact about protective hugs: verbal communication is not necessary. Taking the time to gently hold someone says it all. The other day I gave a routine hug, but the child would not let go. We hugged for a few seconds longer without any words said. But something was loudly communicated by that hug: "You are important and I care about you."

In today's world, physical touching can very quickly become tragic. If someone mistakes the meaning of physical contact, untold problems can occur. This is a scary concept for educators because we work each day with children who outwardly demand or secretly desire hugs. When I was a first-year teacher (24 years old), one of my students, a 16 year old girl, was crying in the hallway. She asked for a hug. Acutely aware of social and professional ramifications, I told that I cared for her but that she would have to settle for a "mental hug." At the time, I saw this as the safe thing to do. I now look back on it as a missed opportunity to share God's love.

Paul tells us that we should express our love for one another:

*My prayer for you is that you will overflow more and more with love for others, and at the same time keep on growing in spiritual knowledge and insight.*
Philippians 1:9 (TLB)

How can we overflow with love for one another and not show it through gentle touches or hugs? Let's never give up on showing love for one another. It is my hope and prayer that if we touch others out of love and concern, that God will protect us from false accusations.

Dear Father,

Thank You for putting us in a situation where we can share Your love daily with Your children. Help us to be aware of others' needs and to always be ready to express Your love with opened arms. Please protect us from harm as we show Your love to others.
Amen

CHAPTER 3

# OCTOBER

October is a month for getting into a routine. We have established our rules and procedures, and the students have had time to acclimate themselves to the teachers and with one another.

It is also a time to get to know the parents. The first grading period ends during October. We now know the students well enough to conference with parents about their needs. It is our duty to get in contact with the parents of each student and give them our assessment of where their child is academically. Phone calls, newsletters, personal notes, and parent conferences are easy ways to show parents that you are dedicated to their child's success. It is imperative to get a positive contact in before something negative occurs. Here is a chance to show God's love and your dedication to His children by involving their parents. Be sure the parents know that God is working through your life.

Fun activities such as Homecoming, Fall Festivals, and Halloween keep us busy. We also concentrate on activities such as Fire Prevention Week, Red Ribbon Week (drug abuse prevention), National School Lunch Week, and School Bus Safety Week. These activities help us to focus on our often overlooked food service workers and bus drivers. Usually in October there are so many activities going on that we get frustrated and wonder, "When are we supposed to teach?" Keep in mind that these activities stick in the children's minds for the rest of their lives. Unfortunately they do not remember our day-to-day learning routines.

The changing leaves and onset of colder weather gives this month a special flavor. We begin to curl up with good books on weekends instead of looking for outdoor activities. This is a good time to reflect again on our guiding principles. We are the shining lights that lead the way for God's children. Continue to ask God for His strength, wisdom and peace.

## A Lesson from Mother Nature

The other day at a red light, I witnessed a bird swooping down on each car as it entered the intersection. I wondered what this "crazy" bird was doing until I noticed an exact replica lying very still in the middle of the intersection. I realized this bird was trying to protect its mate who was seriously injured or dead. Imagine the determination of this several-ounce bird as it charged these moving vehicles weighing several thousand pounds each! I know this bird didn't fully understand the situation, but it had no problem challenging objects much bigger than itself. This bird illustrated to me the definition of true determination: courageously going up against great odds to achieve a purpose!

We as educators sometimes battle against great odds. We are often confronted with children who do not want to learn or behave. Many of them have severe learning or physical disabilities that create great challenges. Educators often receive confusing information regarding curriculum development and instructional techniques. Many have to work with a shortage of equipment and supplies, or within inadequate facilities. To add to our frustrations, we are often criticized by society for not working miracles fast enough. As hopeless as some of these situations may seem, we continue to do what we know is right. I admire educators for their determination, drive and service spirit. I see it in them every day!

Paul tells us about winning attitudes:

> *In a race, everyone runs but only one person gets first prize. So run your race to win.*
>
> 1 Corinthians 9:24 (TLB)

Paul says that if we are in the race, we should be in it to win. There is no doubt that we are in a race for our children's futures. We compete against the many exciting activities that society has to offer. We are often tempted to give up because of the great odds against us. But by dropping out of the race, we will never experience the thrill of victory as we win our children for God.

Miracles cannot happen through us if we do not try. Alone, we do not have the power to perform miracles, but with God's help nothing is impossible. Faith in God (even a small amount - the size of a mustard seed) is the key to moving mountains.

Jesus tells us that we must have faith:

> *Then Jesus told them, "Truly, if you have faith, and don't doubt, you can do things like this and much more. You can even say to this Mount of Olives, 'Move over into the ocean,' and it will."*
>
> Matthew 21:21 (TLB)

Our faith in God is all we need to perform miracles for His children. Be a winner! Trust God and keep charging those moving vehicles!

Dear Father,
Thank You for putting us in such an important profession. Keep us filled with the service spirit so that we never give up. Running the race to win Your children is enough reason to give 100% all of the time. Help us to continue to move those mountains and charge those vehicles!

Amen

## TIME FOR TRIFOCALS

As we work in our classrooms or work places, we must look at all problems that arise through our trifocals. We must consider our own point of view as well as our students' and our parents' as we study these problems and search for solutions. If we are able to do this, we will save ourselves a countless number of headaches.

Many times I have looked at a problem from another point of view, and I was able to gain understanding. Once I was trying to deal with a child who had severe emotional problems. He would curse and strike out at other children as well as adults. Despite numerous testimonies regarding this child's behavior, the parents stood firm that their child would never curse or become violent. I was at a loss! They never would admit to a problem, much less attempt to seek a solution. After I donned my trifocals, I came to realize that this was the parents' way of demonstrating unconditional love and loyalty toward their child. This was their way of protecting him. Although the problem was never solved, at least I came to understand why the parents were seemingly so uncooperative.

When approaching a situation, it is important to look through our trifocals to examine it from all sides. One can look through trifocals by following these steps:

1. Listen to all perceptions.
2. Accept these perceptions as real to the people who own them.
3. Let the others know that you understand their feelings and that you care about them.
4. Work together on a solution.

These steps will be helpful when trying to understand children, teenagers, or adults.

Paul tells us how to treat one another :

*And now this word to all of you: You should be like one big happy family, full of sympathy toward each other, loving one another with tender hearts and humble minds.*

1 Peter 3:8 (TLB)

Being like one big happy family is a quite tall order these days. A family of several billion members will be hard to keep happy, but we can give it a try. No doubt tenderness and humility will go a long way to help us get along.

Dear Father,
Fill us with sympathy, love, and understanding toward one another. We will strive to keep a tender heart and a humble mind as we approach our problems and seek solutions.

Amen

## DIGNITY

The three guiding principles that I try to live by are dignity, service and excellence. To me dignity is the most important because without it, the other two cannot exist. Studies show that once stripped of dignity, a person cannot and will not learn. The brain shuts down as one prepares to defend oneself. Under these conditions, communication comes to a halt and relationships are severed. Therefore, without dignity, the principles of service and excellence cannot exist.

Maintaining students' dignity means treating them like we want to be treated. This means using gentle words and giving freedom with responsibility. It means using caring attitudes and words. It means fun and laughter. It means feeling important and developing friendships. These are things that we adults want. If they are good enough for us, they are good enough for our children. Dignity is not speaking or acting out of anger. It is not over-controlling children. It is not being unfeeling or uncaring. One thing I have learned over the years is that parents will forgive us for not being super-perfect educators, but they will not forgive us for acting like we don't care about their children. Once parents have decided that we don't care, no amount of talk can save the relationship.

Allowing fellow adults to maintain their dignity is just as important. Often times it means keeping one's mouth closed. Words hastily spoken in anger always hurt us. Speaking against each other erodes team spirit and hurts everyone. The best approach is a private, face-to-face conversation with the intent of solving the problem. If approached in a calm, positive, constructive manner, everyone can win. Only if we retain our own dignity and allow others their dignity, can we truly work together and support each other.

Paul tells us to encourage and build each other up:

> *So encourage each other to build each other up,*
> *just as you also are doing.*
> 1 Thessalonians 5:11 (TLB)

> *Let's please the other fellow, not ourselves, and do what*
> *is for his good and thus build him up in the Lord.*
> Romans 15:2 (TLB)

We are told to spend our time and efforts serving and building up our fellow man. We are in the perfect position to dignify many people: students, parents, co-workers, and community members. By upholding the dignity of others and ourselves, we can ensure a successful learning environment for our children.

Dear Father,

Help us to always maintain our own dignity while we preserve the dignity of others. Thank You for supportive colleagues. Together we can build a caring, supportive, and successful learning environment for Your children.

Amen

## DON'T DRIVE INTO THE SMOKE

Once while driving through Oklahoma I kept seeing road signs that said, "Don't Drive Into the Smoke." Never seeing these signs before, I was puzzled. I soon realized that grass fires must be somewhat common in Oklahoma and the signs are reminding motorists of the hazards of driving through the near zero visibility of smoke. These signs were stating the obvious. So why don't we see signs like "Don't Drive into Fire" or "Don't Drive Into Lake," or "Don't Drive Into Brick Walls?" Obvious advice can often sound funny.

All of our lives, we are given obvious advice. People who are risk- takers do not follow everyone's advice. They strike out on their own against all odds. This action calls for great faith in God, others and self. In order for us to have great faith, we need to feel that we are not alone or unprotected.

David sang long ago about the Lord's protection:

*But Lord, you are my shield, my glory, and my only hope.*
Psalms 3:3 (TLB)

As educators, we often avoid taking risks for fear of failure, ridicule, or retaliation. We feel more secure if we hang back and watch the brave ones stick their necks out. However, we are told over and over by the Bible that God's protection is limitless. As we work within God's will, we do not need to worry about taking risks. We can be confident that when we work through God, our successes will be greater than expected.

Christopher Columbus was a risk-taker. He challenged the odds and sailed away to find a new trade route to the Indies. He had faith in God and in himself. God rewarded him for his faith and risk-taking. God blessed him by allowing him to discover a new world!

Dear Father,

You are our strength and our shield. Thank You for the protection that frees our minds from worry. Help us to take risks and conquer this world for Your children.

Amen

## Parent Conferences

Imagine a child in the center of an old rickety step-bridge that stretches across a deep ravine. The bridge is about to collapse and the child needs help. The child's parents enter the bridge from one end. The educators enter from the other, and they meet in the middle. They discuss how to help the child off of the bridge, but they cannot come to an agreement. As they talk, they slowly back away from the child. Eventually, the parents and the educators are yelling at each other from opposite sides of the ravine. As they point fingers at each other, the bridge collapses and the child falls. All that is left to do is to look at one another and blame the others for the loss of the child. It is obvious that in these scenarios nobody wins!

We often get into battles just like this one. We, as educators, know the educational research and have numerous background experiences with children. We want the parents to sit back and listen to our vast professional knowledge. The parents have personal knowledge about their individual child. They know their children better than anyone, and they want to be heard. Many of the disagreements that parents and educators have are not over educational issues; they are about who has the most power. The real issues often get lost in the battles for power.

Parenting and teaching are equally tough jobs. Educators with children know this to be true. Everyone is a stake holder and needs to be part of the decisions at school. Shared decision-making is difficult to achieve because both parents and educators hesitate to relinquish the power of their positions.

Christ told us that those who are humble will receive the greatest of rewards:

> *"Humble men are very fortunate, for the kingdom of Heaven is given to them."*
> 
> Matthew 5: 3 (TLB)

Paul tells us that we are to cooperate with one another:

> *Honor Christ by submitting to each other.*
> 
> Ephesians 5:21 (TLB)

Through a spirit of humbleness and cooperation, we can form the alliances between parents and schools that will lead to successful partnerships. We need to form these partnerships in order to achieve "wins" for the children. Only through these partnerships can we truly become excellent schools.

Dear Father,

We know that we are not the experts in everything. Help us to keep an open mind and to allow others a role in making our many decisions. Your children are the ones who will benefit from our partnerships.

Amen

## HELLO WORLD

Isn't it funny that as educators we already know what our greatest problem is, yet we don't do anything about it? Our most serious fault is also our greatest asset: *we don't let go*! We eat, sleep, think, and breathe education. We talk about education until our spouses and friends beg us to change the subject. We focus so much on our work that we become consumed, and we subject ourselves to early burn-out.

We try to stay positive, but let's face it, our conversations about education are often negative in nature. Since this is the case, no wonder we burn out! If we are constantly subjected to negativity, we will eventually turn sour. I once heard of a principal who adamantly refused to talk education while on break, at lunch, or outside the school. What a gutsy move he made in an attempt to have a life outside of education!

It is important that we change our focus when we are away from work. There is a great big beautiful world out there that doesn't revolve around education. Say hello to it! Plan other activities for yourself during the week such as involvement in church and community organizations, fellowship with friends, hobbies, sports, etc. These life-enhancing activities may serve to save you from education burn-out.

Jesus tells us how to beat burn-out:

> *"Come to me and I will give you rest - all of you who work so hard beneath a heavy yoke."*
>
> Matthew 11:28 (TLB)

Our Lord promises to give us respite from the weariness of the world if we will hand our lives over to Him. He knows how hard we work, and He wants to shelter us from burn-out! All we have to do is go to Him.

Dear Father,
We know that You will give us rest. We are sometimes weary from the hard work of serving Your children. Remind us to seek a life outside of education and to come to You for rest.

Amen

## RIGHT ACTION - WRONG REASON

One day at a movie theater a large, hairy, scruffy-looking man sat down right in front of my wife just as the lights began to dim for the previews. As it was impossible to see over or around his large hair and cowboy hat, my wife politely asked him if he would mind removing his hat. Without even looking at her, he grumbled "No, I ain't gonna move my hat." My wife leaned back and looked at me as I mentally considered my options. I could:

1. Pull his hat off of his head for him.
2. Say something equally rude.
3. Speak to him regarding his rudeness and uncaring attitude.
4. Quietly get up and move.

With great restraint, I chose to move and we shifted over several chairs (there were plenty of seats from which to choose because the theater was only half-full).

Later as I reflected over this incident, I was annoyed with myself that I didn't confront this man over his selfish attitude. I thought that he needed to be told how rude his behavior was, but I needed to avoid a scene. It was pretty obvious to me that any action on my part would have ended in confrontation. I could see the headlines the next morning: "Local Principal Arrested for Brawling in Family Movie Theater." This was not the kind of behavior our community looks for in the leaders of their children, so I moved to another seat. I told myself that I did the right thing.

I now realize that I did the right thing, but for the wrong reason. I avoided a confrontation out of fear of tarnishing my reputation. I should have avoided a confrontation out of kindness toward the large, hairy man. I should have felt compassion for him because of his sadness and anger towards the world. In his own way, he was crying out for help, and I was too concerned with my own reputation to help him.

We are constantly telling our students to do the right thing because it's right, not from fear of punishment for doing wrong. We want them to follow our society's laws out of understanding and respect rather than avoiding punishment. However, we don't always follow that advice. How many of us stay within the speed limit or buckle-up mostly to avoid a traffic ticket?

We are told throughout the Bible to do what is right, but Paul carries it a little further:

> *Keep a close watch on all you do and think. Stay true to what is right and God will bless you and use you to help others.*
>
> 1 Timothy 4:16 (TLB)

We are promised that God will bless us and use us to help others if we remain true to doing what is right. This means we are blessed by God if our intentions are true to His will, and God knows our intentions! We cannot afford to lose this blessing because we are charged to help others while here on this Earth, and we need God's help to do so.

Dear Father,

Please give us the patience, strength, and self-control that we need to avoid unnecessary confrontations. Also help us to match the right attitudes with the right actions.

Amen

## PASS IT ON

Have you ever wondered what your purpose is here on Earth? It is hard to focus on one purpose in life when there are so many different directions our lives can take. We are faced with many decisions and options. Our freedom to choose our own fate often confuses us and leads us to ponder our ultimate destiny. Even with freedom of choice and multiple directions in which to journey, everyone has a single most-important purpose in life. We are here to play a simple child's game called "Pass It On." Only we don't play the game by passing on trivial words or actions, we pass on God's love. We know that others need to experience God's love, and we are anxious to share His love.

Our task as educators is to teach children. Our mission as a child of God is to share His love. Jesus told us of the greatest commandment:

> *Jesus replied, "'Love the Lord your God with all your heart, soul, and mind.' this is the first and greatest commandment. The second most important is similar: 'Love your neighbor as much as you love yourself.'"*
>
> Matthew 22:37-39 (TLB)

We are in the perfect position to teach children to love God, to love others, and to love themselves. "Teach children to love God?" you ask. "Not in a public school, thank you very much! Don't forget separation of Church and State!" Our wise forefathers knew that religious freedom would be impossible if the government controlled our religious practices. In our usual confused manner, we have almost made it a crime to talk about God to our children in public schools. However, it is not a crime to show God's love to His children. In fact we are specifically charged to do just that:

> *Little children, let us stop just saying we love people; let us really love them, and show it by our actions.*
>
> 1 John 3:18 (TLB)

It is not a crime to act as a Christian and share God's love by teaching the children values such as courage, conviction, respect, courtesy, honesty, patience, truth, responsibility, thoughtfulness, and self-discipline. Everything we do and say each day should reflect our love for God and our desire to share His love with others:

> *And whatever you do or say, let it be as a representative of the Lord Jesus*
>
> Colossians 3:17 (TLB)

Even though it is not always accepted, we must do what is right. We are charged to spread God's love to everyone around us. We are privileged to play the ultimate "Pass It On" game here on Earth. And our profession gives us the perfect playing field!

Dear Father,
Thank You for Your perfect love. Help us to pass that love on to others every minute of each day.

Amen

## COFFEE, TEA, OR TECHNOLOGY?

One morning I was enjoying an excellent breakfast and good conversation with a waitress at a local restaurant. We were talking about the evolution of service in America. She pointed to the coffee urn at the table as an example of how service has changed. She stated that the coffee urn provides the customer with the convenience of immediate coffee refills, but it reduces the interaction between waitresses and customers. She said that she missed the conversations that often resulted from her refilling customers' coffee cups. I see this an example of how our society is slowly "conveniencing" itself right out of human relationships. In our efforts to automate service, we are drastically reducing our interactions with one another.

One reason for a reduction in human interaction and relationship-building is technology. I think we can all agree that technology is a great thing, and that it is improving our lives in many ways. It allows for faster service, faster business transactions, faster communications, etc. However, technology is also responsible for a serious decline in the quality of human relations. Have any of your relationships been hampered by television, stereos, fax machines, video games, computers, or the internet?

The rapid speed of interaction created by technology does not give us time to get to know one another well. Without these prolonged personal interactions, strong relationships cannot be built or maintained. Technology also reduces our need to meet one another face-to-face. We no longer need to personally interact with bank tellers, gas station attendants, phone receptionists, pharmacists, etc. It is easier to be indifferent toward people with whom we are not in close contact (I find it far easier to hang up the phone than I do to shut the door). When we find ourselves face-to-face with others, we tend to be more compassionate and empathetic. I believe that this loss of quality personal interaction is devastating to our relationship-building processes.

Can technology and quality human relationships co-exist? Of course! But it will take an extra effort on our part to see that technology does not replace our desire to personally know and serve one another.

James tells us why we should commit to one another right away and not wait until later:

> *For what is your life? It is even a vapor that appears*
> *for a little time and then vanishes away.*
> James 4:14 (NKJV)

As James so aptly puts it, our lives here on Earth are extremely short. We have precious little time to establish our relationships, serve others, and prepare for our eternal life with God. Technology can either help or hinder our efforts to serve one another. We make the decision. Be on the lookout for ways that technology helps or hinders your personal interactions and relationship-building.

Dear Father,

    Thank You for life here on Earth. Although our time here is short, we can still strive to perfect our relationships with one another. Help us to value each minute as we share Your love with others.

Amen

## CHAPTER 4

# NOVEMBER

November is a month for continued relationship-building with students, parents, and colleagues. A special emphasis on family, friendship, and thankfulness is brought to us through the holidays of Thanksgiving and Veteran's Day. This month gives us a great opportunities to model God's grace and teach children to be thankful for God's blessings.

Election Day, Youth Appreciation Week, American Education Week, National Geography Awareness Week, an National Children's Book Week all offer good excuses to do something different and exciting for the students.

The newness of the school year has definitely worn off at this point. We are well into our established pattern. The first twinges of burn-out can begin to hit. Be sure to wear your trifocals and look at all situations through other points of view. Also remember to play "Pass it on" and keep charging those moving vehicles! I am sure that God is pleased with our hard work and sacrifice as we help raise His children.

The December holiday celebrations are beginning to loom ever more closely. The stores are all well-stocked by now, and the spirit of the season is upon us. After the Thanksgiving holidays it is even more of a challenge to keep the students focused. This month is an important part of their "academic climb" because we are preparing to close out the first semester of school, and the students need a final push to succeed. However, many students don't seem to understand or appreciate the importance of this final push. Keep in constant touch with God. Let Him know what you need in order to best serve His children.

## SURELY YOU JEST

Do you laugh with your students? Do you pull pranks, act silly, dress up in costumes, dance, sing songs, or tell jokes? Do you do the unexpected? Do you lie on the floor, sit on the desks, and sometimes break the rules? Do your students think sometimes that you have taken leave of your senses? If you do these things, you do them because you enjoy kids. You know that you have to be wild and crazy to get the students' attention and get them interested in what you want them to do.

In order to do these things, you have to like yourself as well as your students. You have to be spontaneous and choose to have fun. You also have to be self-assured and willing to expose your vulnerable self. You have to be humble and able to laugh at yourself. In other words, you have to have a sense of humor.

Our children thrive on humor. Look at how much they laugh with one another! We think that most of their humor is off-base, but it belongs to them. They constantly incorporate humor into everything they do. I am sorry to say that we tend to lose our humor as we grow older and get serious about life.

We are told what a sense of humor will do for us:

> *A merry heart does good, like medicine, But a broken spirit dries the bones.*
>
> Proverbs 17:22 (NKJV)

A merry heart will keep us healthy and happy, but without it we tend to "dry-up." Perhaps your life needs some medicine and nothing seems to be working. Give humor a try. A good way to get started is to pick up some books on humor and look at life through the eyes of humorists. They have a great way of minimizing problems through laughter.

Shake your students up by hitting them with some unexpected humor. They will be delighted!

Dear Father,

Thank You for humor. It is what keeps us healthy, happy, and alive. Help us not to outgrow humor. We will strive to keep a merry heart as we serve Your children.

Amen

## CRYING OVER SPILT CHILDREN

My preacher asked an interesting question one Sunday, "When did you last cry over the loss of someone?" He wasn't referring to a person's death, but to their being lost. I couldn't help but think of the difficult children that I have encountered throughout my career. Many of them were lost because of their upbringing. Through no fault of their own, they developed poor attitudes toward themselves, others, and life in general. As a result, they were not very lovable or even likable.

I wish I had cried over these students. Instead, I got angry at them for the things that they did. The easiest way to deal with them was removal from the classroom. This allowed them to be isolated and punished while the rest of the students continued with their educations. Once removed, these "trouble makers" could be forgotten for a while. If everyone was lucky, they would move away or drop out before they came back to class.

I am sure Jesus often cried over what He saw. Many of the people he came across must have caused him great sadness because they had strayed so far from His Father's will. Yet, he stayed with them and told them how important they were to His Father. He also showed them how much they meant to Him by comforting their sorrows and being with them. Our God, the King of Kings, spent time with the lowest of mortal man. He was criticized often for this, but He knew the importance of showing everyone that they were worthy of His love and attention.

Jesus demonstrated this perfect love to me, yet I refused to spend a small amount of time trying to help some of His troubled children. It was too easy to overlook these children and focus on those students who showed more promise. Perhaps I could have made a difference in their lives if I had taken the time to cry.

Jesus tells us why it is important not to ignore those in need:

> *"When you refused to help the least of these, my brothers, you were refusing help to me."*
>
> Matthew 25: 45 (TLB)

It saddens me to think that at times I have turned away from Jesus and refused to help His children. Fortunately God forgives us and each day is a new opportunity for us to serve His children. Perhaps it doesn't pay to cry over spilt milk, but crying over "spilt" children can make all the difference in the world.

Dear Father,
We are sorry that we haven't cried more than we have over lost children. Please forgive us for our missed opportunities. Help us to recognize when Your children need help and give us the wisdom and patience to work with them.

Amen

## **WHERE IS THE GRATITUDE?**

How often are you thanked for what you do? My guess is not very often. You most likely get a thank you now and then from colleagues if your working relationship is good. If you are lucky, you hear occasionally from your boss that you are doing a good job. On rare occasions parents will write a letter or tell your supervisors about your dedication and hard work. If you are really fortunate, you will hear from a student years later that you made a real difference in his or her life. This is hardly enough encouraging feedback for people who totally devote their lives to helping others.

As humans we are fueled by acknowledgements and praise. We need a "thank you" as much as a car needs gas. If we do not feel recognized or appreciated, we have a hard time getting revved-up for the job! Eventually, we can run out of gas and quit entirely.

I have heard it expressed that educators are like buckets of praise. Their job is to build children up by constantly showering them with praise and attention. Once educators' buckets have been emptied, they need to be refilled. What does it take to keep refilling these buckets? Portions of these buckets can be refilled with intrinsic positive self-worth. Educators who know they work hard and get good results can partially refill their own buckets. But what of the remaining portions of these buckets? If they must be refilled by praise from others, we could be in for a long wait.

Jesus tells us not to look for praise because we have only done our duty:

> *"So likewise you, when you have done all those things which you are commanded, say 'We are unprofitable servants. We have done what was our duty to do.'"*
>
> Luke 17:10 (NKJV)

If we are serving the Lord, we are not to waste time seeking praise from people. These activities are no longer necessary to keep our buckets full. God does this for us. God provides us with a bucket that never empties. We will never run out of energy as long as we serve God and His children!

Although we should not seek praise for ourselves, we should spend time and effort building up those around us. Let's select some people that we work with and praise them for serving others. Let's provide some fuel for our fellow educators!

Dear Father,

Thank You for providing us with a never ending bucket of praise that nourishes our children and replenishes us. Please keep us refueled so that we may accomplish Your will.

Amen

## IN A CHILD'S SHOES

Children have a different way of looking at life than we do. I discover this over and over again. One of my first days on the job as an elementary school assistant principal (newly arrived from the high school world), a child came to me in tears. He said, "Mr. Stephen, Anthony cut me!" Looking for blood, I asked him where he was hurt! I came to find that the "cut" was someone getting in front of him in line. Another day at another school, a child came to the front office looking for the principal. One of the secretaries pointed to the principal of the school (who was a woman) and said, "There is the principal. She is right here." The little girl looked at her in frustration and said, "No, not her. I want the 'boy' principal!" And one day I got a love note from one of my students that said, "Dear Mr. Stephen, I love you for a principal ........... you make a good one for your age!" I am never lacking for good stories that come from the eyes and mouths of the children. They certainly think differently than we do.

This difference in thinking, however, can create problems. For example, one of the toughest situations for educators in trying to teach the 3 R's to students is that the students are interested in the 3 F's: Food, Fun, and Friends. It is difficult to capture and maintain students' attention while they are focusing on these 3 F's. I asked a girl one time what she would do if she were to become the principal. Her reply was that she would play music over the PA, serve better food, and have more recess. I asked her about the curriculum and student performance on standardized tests, and she said that she would worry about that later.

Students have a tremendous need for the 3 F's. At times it seems they will go to any lengths to avoid the 3 R's in order to continue their search for food, fun, and friends. To fully understand their wants and needs, we must walk in their shoes. This is not easy. Their shoes are too small, and they are uncomfortable to get into. Getting inside of a child's mind also takes effort and discomfort. As difficult as it is, we must tailor our instruction to the interests of our students.

Jesus tells us the importance of understanding children and imitating them:

> *"Therefore, anyone who humbles himself as this little child, is the greatest in the Kingdom of Heaven."*
> Matthew 18:4 (TLB)

Jesus tells us that there are great advantages to thinking like a child. By humbling ourselves and trying to understand His children, we are elevated in the Kingdom of Heaven!

Dear Father,
We are Your children who are serving Your children. Help us to love, protect and understand Your children as much as You love, protect and understand us.

Amen

## BE QUICK TO LISTEN

When someone comes to us with a problem, how do we react? While he is talking, do we ...........

> daydream about something else?
> contemplate our own problems?
> Mentally go over our "to do" list?
> think of advice that we can give?
> formulate the perfect answer?
> interrupt him before he finishes?

These are some perfectly normal responses that we make when we are asked to listen. As a result, maybe we have heard this person's problems, but we have not really listened!

Hearing what someone says to us is easy. Listening to someone is difficult. What is the difference? When we truly listen, we tune into feelings as well as words. In a way, we listen with our hearts, not our ears. We truly listen by climbing into someone else's shoes and walking around in them.

Jesus summed it up well by saying:

> *"Try to show as much compassion as your Father does."*
> Luke 6:36 (TLB)

After people speak, they may or may not ask for advice. Many times children, parents, or fellow educators simply want to get something off of their minds. They want to bounce an idea or situation off of someone to see how it sounds. People tend to look for listeners when they need help. They are not necessarily looking for advice givers.

One day a student asked me what I do all day as a principal. I thought for a moment and said, "I talk and listen all day long." In a nutshell that is what educators do - they communicate. Listening is far more important than talking when it comes to effective communication. We have all found that students and parents want to be listened to - not talked to.

We are given excellent advice on how to interact with others from James:

> *So then, my beloved brethren, let every man be swift to hear, slow to speak, slow to wrath; for the wrath of man does not produce the righteousness of God.*
> James 1: 19-20 (NKJV)

What great advice this is! Be quick to listen and slow to anger. Arguments would be impossible if everyone concentrated on listening rather than talking. Think of what our schools would be like if every person made a special effort to listen to others and not get angry .......... it would truly be Heaven on Earth!

Dear Father,
    Remind us that listening is far better than talking. We often forget this. Help us to be quick to listen and slow to anger so that we might pass this on to Your children.

Amen

## IN THE EYES OF THE BEHOLDER

Children watch us very closely. Every move we make is a model for them to see. They are formulating their personalities and the character traits that they will live by for the rest of their lives, and they are learning from our examples every day. What tremendous pressure that puts on us! Since children are using our lives as patterns, we must lead near perfect lives! How can we do that? We can't be perfect, so what is the most important quality for us to model?

Paul tells us what he believes should be our focal point:

> *And above all things have fervent love for one another, for love will cover a multitude of sins.*
>
> 1 Peter 4:8 (NKJV)

Isn't it great to know that if we concentrate on showing love for others, that this will cover up our "multitude" of sins? This is true in our schools. We educators certainly are not perfect, however children do not notice all of our faults because they know that we love and care for them. We are constantly amazed with the high esteem in which our students hold us because we know that we are loaded down with a multitude of faults. It is good that our loving attitudes are able to cloak these faults in the eyes of our students!

Think of a teacher that you appreciated as you were growing up. Think of all of the reasons you liked this teacher. Now think of this teacher's faults. Most likely you can't think of any. You overlooked the teacher's faults because you were loved.

Our relationships with our peers work the same way. We are mature and aware enough to know that our colleagues are not perfect. However, we tend to overlook the sins of one another if we believe that we are loved. It is love that holds us together and keeps us working cooperatively.

Dear Father,

Thank You for the love that binds and blinds! Please help us to demonstrate this love to those around us.

Amen

## RIGHT AT THE END OF YOUR NOSE

Many answers in life are obvious. They are right at the end of our noses. So why don't we always see them? Sometimes we can't see the simplest of solutions to our challenges because we are too close to the situation. We often have a personal stake or personal involvement that prevents us from seeing the situation clearly. Our tunnel vision often restricts our view of the problem; therefore the range of solutions is also restricted. Quite often we need to step back from our situations and examine the obvious.

So how do we do this? We can slow down and allow time for ourselves to examine the problem and possible solutions. Sometimes patience over a period of time allows for problems to work themselves out. Another possibility is to ask someone else for advice or insights into the problem. Sometimes another perspective is all that is needed to see the obvious solution. I can't tell you how many times I have asked someone for a solution only to receive a strange look because the solution was so obvious!

The never-fail solution is to ask God for His intervention. Paul told us almost two thousand years ago:

> *If you want to know what God wants you to do, ask him, and He will gladly tell you, for He is always ready to give a bountiful supply of wisdom to all who ask him*
> 
> James 1:5 (TLB)

God tells us to simply be aware that He is God, that He knows what is best, and that He will give us the answers. All we need to do is go to Him for the solutions to our problems.

Dear Father,
You have the answers to all of our problems. Give us the wisdom to seek Your guidance.

Amen

## LISTEN TO GOD

When do you do your best thinking? My best thinking is done in the shower. It is quiet, steamy, warm, and comfortable in my shower. Given time, I can solve problems, formulate new ideas, and set the agenda for the day. If I had a waterproof pen and paper, I could stay in the shower longer (much to the dismay of my wife and our electric bill) and solve the problems of the entire world.

Our best thinking is done in meditative silence. Screening out the world and its problems is a must when focusing on problem-solving or planning for the future. Before we can focus on the big picture, we have to empty our minds of the "trivial pursuits" that distract us.

I hear God best when I am silent. He speaks to me in solitude. It is my responsibility to arrange this time for meditation. If I don't, I am choosing not to listen to what God has to say. This is when things begin to go wrong for me. When I listen to myself or rely upon my own abilities, I am cutting out the greatest help that exists. God is always with us and ready to help, but we must call upon Him.

God's answer on how to meditate is the simplest of all:

> *Be still and know that I am God.*
>
> Psalm 46:10 (NKJV)

Notice that God did not say, "Try to slow down and be relatively convinced that I am God." He tells us that if we stop and give Him our complete attention, we will know beyond any doubt that He is God. This assurance will provide us the peace that we need in this world.

Inspiration comes and goes. Grab it when you can!

Dear Father,

Help us to seek solitude and listen to You. We need Your inspiration in order to best serve Your children.

Amen

## CHAPTER 5

# DECEMBER

December is definitely a different kind of month. It signifies the end of the semester for some of us. It holds one of the most celebrated and joyous of holidays. It also provides a rest for educators in the form of mid-year vacation. We take time for ourselves and our families during this break from work. A spirit of loving, giving, and sharing pervades our thinking during this month. Our traditions and celebrations provide us with a distraction from the every day occurrences of our school life.

This month also marks the first day of Winter. The cold weather and possibility of snow sparks thoughts of chestnuts roasting, hot chocolate, carolers, silver bells and sleigh rides. Once again family takes over in our thoughts and deeds (this includes frantic gift buying before the stores close).

Even though family and friends take much of our attention this month, don't forget your students and colleagues. Ask those around you how they are and stick around to listen to their answer. Be there if they need to talk. Walk in their shoes and feel their situations. Crying over our unlovable children means that we are seeing them through God's eyes. Remember we are here to serve all of God's children - not just the easy ones.

A hectic, manic, frantic pace followed by peaceful, blissful, cheerful relaxation is the oxymoron called "December." Indulge yourself and your family during this wonderful season. But do not forget the true reason behind the season: God's greatest gift - Jesus Christ, His only son our Lord.

## HERE TO SERVE

I remember years ago a phone company advertised themselves as "The Only Phone Company in Town, but We Try Not to Act Like It." I always wondered if that was true. The horror of the consumer world is that companies will gain monopolies, inflate prices, and reduce quality of service. With no competition, consumers would be totally at their mercy.

I wonder if some educational systems might have this nightmare-type attitude: "Since we are the only public school system in town, we do not need to worry about customer satisfaction. If the students and parents are unhappy, it is too bad because we have always done it this way and we are not going to change." This kind of attitude is far from a service attitude. It is an attitude of arrogance and indifference.

In the consumer world, attitudes like this would cause businesses to lose customers and go out of business. So why should educators worry about running off customers? Public schools can't go out of business! We still must be concerned about customer satisfaction because when we "lose a customer," we turn a student away from learning and the opportunity to reap the long-term benefits of a good education. We don't go out of business, but we can ruin a life.

We cannot afford to exhibit arrogance or indifference as we work with our children and their parents. We must exhibit an attitude of service. We must be genuinely humble. Service must be in our hearts and minds. A service attitude will help us to gain the trust of our children and their parents. Then perhaps, they will honor us for the service that we perform. If not, the joy of serving others is still ours. No one can take that away.

Jesus tells us how important a service attitude is:

> *And whoever of you desires to be first shall be slave of all. For even the Son of Man did not come to be served, but to serve, and to give His life a ransom for many.*
>
> Mark 10: 44-45 (NKJV)

There is no doubt that we are expected to serve one another here on Earth. Moreover, we are to *humbly* serve one another. We are told of both the dangers of honoring ourselves and the rewards of humbleness:

> *For everyone who tries to honor himself shall be humbled; and he who humbles himself shall be honored.*
>
> Luke 14:11 (TLB)

Jesus Christ provided the perfect example of what true service is. He humbled Himself as He served us here on Earth, even to the point of total self-sacrifice. His charge to us is to become as Christ-like as possible. We are to humbly serve other to the best of our ability, even to the point of self-sacrifice. The education profession provides us an excellent vehicle in which to humbly serve God and His children.

Dear Father,

Thank You for leading us to the profession in which we can make a great difference in Your children's futures. Help us to maintain a service attitude as we educate Your children. Give us the strength to be humble toward others. As we are aware of Your sacrifice for us, help us to sacrifice ourselves for others.

Amen

## STOPLIGHTS OF LIFE

I have grown accustomed to waiting a few seconds before I enter an intersection after the light turns green. Quite often someone will run their red light by a full 3 seconds or more. This doesn't sound like much, but it is a tragic accident waiting to happen. It is hard for me to imagine someone so selfish or in enough of a hurry to risk a collision in the middle of an intersection just to save thirty or forty seconds.

Our society is slowly losing its stoplights. People seem more likely to disobey laws today than ever before. As a result, the honest citizens are penalized for the acts of the dishonest citizens. For example, we have to pay for gas up front and we have to show identification to write a check because of other people's dishonesty. Also, anger seems to be at an all-time high. Some people have lost their inner-stoplights that control their anger responses. As a result, we see personal violence on the rise. At times it appears that we are creating a scary world for our children to inherit.

As honest citizens, we can stand up for what is right and fair. We can speak our minds and show the courage to do what is right. We owe it to the next generation to build a better world for tomorrow. We are in an excellent position to teach our nation's children about life's stoplights. We can show them that there are certain boundaries that cannot be crossed without dire consequences. We can also model and teach self-control and self-responsibility to our children. We can teach them to stand up for what is right.

With God's help, we can win the fight against the wrong-doers! King David asked God for help:

*Assign me Godliness and Integrity as my bodyguards,*
*for I expect you to protect me*

Psalms 25:21 (TLB)

Jesus tells us of the rewards of standing up for what is right:

> *"For if you stand firm, you will win your souls."*
> Luke 21:19 (TLB)

With God's help, we can stand up and do what is right. Our real struggle in life is not against people. It is against the evil that people do. With God's strength and protection, we can win our battles against evil. Our pay-off for standing firm is a better life on Earth and an eternal life with God for ourselves and our children.

Dear Father,
With Your help, we can fight the evil that is taking over our world. Help us to stand up and make this a better place for Your children.

Amen

## BE A SHINING LIGHT

Ask yourself this question: "Do educators add to the doom and gloom of society?" Think before you answer because we probably do in some way. It is easy to get caught up in the "negativism" that pervades our world today. Isn't it easy to listen to someone who is spreading some really juicy gossip or get caught up in the fun of lambasting parents who do not raise their children as we would approve? Do we find ourselves criticizing students in front of other educators? Have we ever said "TGIF" or wished for Friday on a Monday?

All of us display negative attitudes at one time or another. Negative thoughts seem to arise easily and naturally. However, negativity can lead to our destruction. To paraphrase what King Solomon once said, "What you think is what you are." The more negative thoughts that invade our lives, the more sour we become. A grumpy old person is created one thought at a time! We even wear our negative thoughts on our faces in the form of dark scowls, frowns, and "poor pitiful me" expressions.

Positive thoughts, on the other hand, tend to lighten one's life. We can actually see that positive thoughts can lighten and cheer one's face. Is there joy in your face? Does your face radiate with the love of God? Are you a shining light to guide others down the correct path in life?

Paul tells us to stay away from complaining and arguing and to be a light shining in a dark world:

> *Do all things without complaining and disputing, that you may become blameless and harmless, children of God without fault in the midst of a crooked and perverse generation, among whom you shine as lights in the world.*
> Philippians 2: 14-15 (NKJV)

God tells us to focus on the joys of life. Look for the joys that surround you. Fill your mind with these positive thoughts and allow them to illuminate your face and your entire life. Other people want you to be negative. They want you to join them in their sorry, negative world. The next time someone tries to pull you down with them into a negative conversation, tell them, "No thanks, I'm trying to cut down!"

Dear Father,
We are Your lights in this world. Help us to shine for others, so they can also find You and Your infinite love.

Amen

## THE BIGGEST PICTURE

We are often criticized because we do not see the "Big Picture." Principals often complain because teachers and staff focus only on their individual classrooms, grade levels, subject areas, or job areas.

Superintendents often complain because principals focus only on their buildings and their students. State level leaders complain that the school superintendents only think of their school districts. Each level of the bureaucracy accuses the others of having tunnel vision.

We are all sometimes guilty of tunnel vision. We can have such a great concern for our own corner of the world that we do not see the big picture of which we are a small part. We might find ourselves saying things like: "They don't care about us......we are just little people," or "They are too busy to be concerned about us," or "They don't understand what it is really like." We can be quite hurt if we feel isolated or unimportant.

Paul tells us that it is important to work together:

*Then make me truly happy by loving each other and agreeing wholeheartedly with each other, working together with one heart and mind and purpose.*
Philippians 2:2 (TLB)

We need to step away from our individual situations and see how everyone works together to create the big picture. At the school level, each employee has individual concerns and difficulties, but everyone works together for the children. At the district level, we can see how all local schools work together to prepare children for entering the community as productive adult citizens. The next step is to see the bigger picture of national education. This involves the intellectual, emotional, spiritual, behavioral, and social growth of our entire nation. If educators work together with one heart, mind and purpose, our states can produce a new generation that will strengthen our nation.

We are now ready to see the biggest picture in education. We are preparing our children to live their lives as God intends. We are creating a more godly nation here on Earth and ensuring eternal life for ourselves and our children. This is the most important, lasting education that we can give our children.

Dear Father,

Never let us forget to focus on the biggest picture in education which is to share Your love and lead others to You. Together we in education can work with one heart, mind and purpose for Your children.

Amen

## Turn Your Creative Juices Loose

I wonder if you are also guilty of my dilemma - I nearly killed my creative side. I discovered my creative side in high school. I enjoyed many adventures and spent hours writing poetry and playing music on oboe and clarinet. I graduated high school and put my "toys" away. I then became very good at studying and making good grades. After college, I became very good at working. At age 24, I prematurely became thirty-something. I threw myself into the professional world and began climbing the corporate ladder. I took work home every night and on weekends. I graded papers and planned lessons with my free time and attended graduate school at night and during the summers. I forgot how to be creative and enjoy the beauty of the world! Recently I have begun playing the oboe and writing poetry again, and I am happier for it! I look forward to the times that I can retreat from work to create music and poetry.

We all have a creative side, and I dare say some of us never discover it. What a travesty that is! God wants us to be creative. He has given each of us the ability to create beauty. We do this in a variety of ways: arts, crafts, writing, music, etc. Being creative is a way of changing the normal everyday work pattern we have set for ourselves.

You too have a creative side. Have you buried it in favor of working? When was the last time you let your creative self go? How creative are you at work? Do you ever allow your creativity to produce change in your professional or personal life?

God tells us to use the creative talents that He gave us:

*God has given each of you some special abilities; be sure to use them to help each other, passing on to others God's many kinds of blessings.*
1 Peter 4:10 (TLB)

Find something to pursue with a passion - something that will rekindle your creative spirit. Do it right away!

Dear Father,
    Thank You for our creative side. Help us not to lock away our creativity in order to save more time for work.
Amen

## THE WEEK BEFORE CHRISTMAS BREAK
(In an elementary school in Texas)

It was the week before Christmas Break
Monday morning, 7:03.
Not a person was stirring
(except our before school program, latch-key.)

The staff soon would be braced at their stations
their hearts filled with excitement (and a little dread)
of the endless activities, wild children, and extra paperwork
that they expected in the week ahead.

Sitting alone in my office, I must admit that I also did try
to wish that this week had already gone by.

When suddenly I heard such a clatter
that I sprang from my desk to see what was the matter.
I saw a gentleman signing for a visitor's badge so quick,
I knew in a moment it must be St. Nick.

Two weeks shy of Christmas, I asked
"Santa, what are you doing here?"
To which he smiled and said,
"I've come to spread some news of good cheer."

He said, "You need a reminder that I can't stress enough.
You spend too much time sweating the little stuff!

This week will be hectic, it is true,
but treasure each moment as it happens to you.
For amidst all of the usual toil and strife
you have a chance to make a difference in a life.

Don't forget the true meaning of Christmas
a reminder of God's gift from above -
the gift of his Son
and His never ending love.

This love is to be shared,
not hoarded inside.
You must wrap your children in it
with your arms opened wide."

Before I could respond, he dashed out into the hall,
saying "Merry Christmas, Happy New Year and
       God bless y'all."

    Isn't it an incredible irony that we educators get so "on edge" during the Christmas Season? The time of year that we are supposed to feel a special peace and good will toward others, and instead, everyone is about to get on one another's last nerve! The combination of our own fatigue and excited children can cause our undoing in regard to Christmas cheer.

Only a focus on the true meaning of Christmas can pull us out of this pre-Christmas nose dive:

> *Then the angel said to them, "Do not be afraid, for behold, I bring you good tidings of great joy which will be to all people. For there is born to you this day in the city of David a Savior who is Christ the Lord."*
>
> Luke 2: 10-11 (NKJV)

Dear Father,

This is a blessed season. Thank You for the birth of Jesus, His supreme sacrifice, and Your gift of everlasting life. Please help us to focus on Your gift and not to fret over trivial things.

Amen

## CHAPTER 6

# JANUARY

January is a month for resolutions and rededication. We make resolutions for our personal and professional lives, and we rededicate ourselves to our ideals and to our students. It is a time to review our personal goals for the year and provide needed adjustments. It is also time to have the students reflect on their accomplishments and communicate their progress to parents.

We are refreshed from our vacation and ready for the second half of the school year. Along with the second semester comes new beginnings once again. We are planning for the new semester or the second half of the year. We are getting new students, and in some cases, new subject areas to teach. God is great help when it comes to new beginnings. Be sure to ask Him for wisdom, strength and peace.

January is a month to focus on our cultural diversity here in the United States. We celebrate our diversity through special events such as the Martin Luther King Day and World Religion Day. Opportunities are provided for us to help us understand that we are unique individuals, yet we are interdependent upon one another. Also, don't forget to celebrate our school nurses on National School Nurse Day. Our "Angels of Mercy" are often overlooked when it comes to gratitude.

## Post-Christmas Vacation Blues

As usual, I was recently struck with the "Post-Christmas Vacation Blues." My thoughts at first were "I can't believe that these two weeks went by so quickly, and I have to go back to work on Monday." However, after deep contemplation, I came to the conclusion that I am glad to go back to work after all. Here are the top ten reasons:

1. I have run out of Christmas money (and the month of January is already looking quite lean).
2. I've opened all of my presents and it doesn't look like I'm getting any more.
3. I have to begin proving to Santa that I deserve a visit from him next Christmas Eve.
4. I cannot afford to totally quit working - my family has this silly habit of requiring food and shelter.
5. I missed being surrounded by talented and caring colleagues.
6. I missed the adoration of the students (my own kids know me too well to adore me).
7. The chores list at home was getting too long, and I was running out of excuses of why I couldn't get to them.
8. I can't wait to see what new projects I will receive from my bosses.
9. I can't wait to see what our state legislature will do to us.
10. My wife needs a break.

Seriously, the true reason that we are glad to be back at work is that we have a mission to serve others. The two week vacation gives us an opportunity to rest, visit with friends and relatives, and do some chores. It is a very self-serving two weeks (and we need it), but we are ready to begin serving our children again.

Paul reminds us why we work:

> *Remember that it is the Lord Christ who is going to pay you, giving you your full portion of all he owns. He is the one you are really working for.*
>
> Colossians 3:24 (TLB)

Our Lord is our true boss. He is the one we are working for and trying to please. We, as educators, have dedicated ourselves to serving God's children. The two-week rest is nice, but we must get back to our calling. Together, let's renew that service spirit that keeps us coming back for more!

Dear Father,
Thank You for the rest. You are our shelter and our shield. Renew us and prepare us to lead Your children according to Your will.

Amen

## NEW YEAR'S RESOLUTIONS

I have taken the burden of New Year's Resolutions away from you this year. You will not need to go through the painful process of self-reflecting and generating numerous resolutions. No need to thank me, it was really Paul that did the thinking for all of us. Since we are chosen by God, Paul says that we must work on the following characteristics to please Him:

Compassion
Kindness
Humility
Patience
Gentleness
Forgiveness
Love
Peace
Thankfulness

These resolutions come from Colossians 3:12-15. Since these are the character traits that the Lord wants us to exhibit, all other resolutions seem to pale in importance. But these characteristics are not easy to exhibit on a constant basis. These traits are especially vulnerable when we are in a hurry. Because these are deliberate actions, we have to give conscious thought and take extra time to show compassion, kindness, gentleness, etc. When pressed for time, it is easier to overlook these actions for the sake of speed and efficiency.

We can slow down and live according to these characteristics. By demonstrating patience, compassion, etc., we are telling others how important they are to us. This is what our students want from us: to know that we think that they are important.

Jesus tells us His expectations for our character:

> *"Therefore you shall be perfect, even as your Father in heaven is perfect."*
>
> Matthew 5:48 (NKJV)

Perfection! This is no small order. Jesus tells us we are to strive for perfection. As you strive for perfection, take the time to exhibit these characteristics outlined in Colossians. This resolution will cost you plenty of time and effort, but the payoff will be enormous. You stand to win your students because they crave this kind of attention from you.

Dear Father,

Thank You for choosing us to be Your servants here on Earth. Thank You for entrusting us with Your children. Please help us as we daily strive for perfection. Help us to slow down and make these traits a natural part of our character. In this way we can show others how important they are to us.

Amen

## Shelter in a Storm

Picture yourself as a warm cozy room with a fireplace, and that some of your students are wanderers in a very cold night. You serve as a refuge, a place to step into from the dark and bitter cold. You are a place where children can warm themselves, regenerate and feel safe for a while.

Some of our children spend their lives in a cold, hard environment. They go through some pretty tough times, and they may begin to wonder if there is any purpose to life. At times they will seek refuge and may need to step into your cozy room for a while. You can warm them up and make them feel better about themselves and the world.

From Student to Teacher:<br>
A Love Poem

There is a room of which I know
that always has a fire aglow.
In it sits a chair all plush
the sounds within are all a hush.

There are blankets to make me cozy and warm
and a bolted door to keep out harm.
The book on the table contains a happy ending
it makes my time well-worth spending.

There is a cup of hot chocolate by the chair
and the smell of fresh baked bread in the air.
How long I stay, I need not worry
because time slows down, there is no hurry.

This room of course is in my mind
the times I enter it are few,
I am mostly in this room I find
when I am close to you.

Our Lord serves as our refuge. As Moses told us:

> "The eternal God is your refuge, and underneath are the everlasting arms."
>
> Deuteronomy 33:27 (NKJV)

Jesus tells us that we are to shelter our children:

> "And any of you who welcomes a little child like this because you are mine, is welcoming me and caring for me."
>
> Matthew 18:5 (TLB)

Just as God serves as our refuge, we are to serve as protectors of His children. Once again we are told that as we serve His children, we are also serving Him. As educators, we are in the perfect position to serve as a refuge for our students.

Dear Father,
Thank You for protecting us and serving as our refuge. Please continue to strengthen us to do the same for Your children.

Amen

## THE PROPER FOCUS

What do you surround yourself with on a daily basis to remind yourself of God and His will for your life? Is it a picture, a poster, a Bible? We all know that it is difficult in a public school setting to surround yourself with items that remind you of God's plan .......... or is it?

I have seen a principal who keeps a Bible right in the middle of his conference table. I have seen teachers' rooms with Biblical sayings posted and pictures on the wall that remind me of God and His beautiful world. I have a poster of the fruits of the spirit on my wall and pictures of lighthouses surrounding my office. These objects remind me of my true purpose. They help me keep my heart and mind on God and His will.

Focus on God? Sure, Sundays are easy! We meet with other godly people and focus on God and his plan for our lives and our world. But Mondays through Fridays are different. We are in a secular setting with some very ungodly people. There are times when we feel far away from God's peace, and we need a support system to lean on throughout the week.

Can you recognize when you are losing God's peace and beginning to fret over the ways of the world? If you do, how do you "reel yourself in" and regain God's peace? Do you have a symbolic rock to hold onto such as a visual Bible verse, a picture on the wall, a song, or a friend?

We are told of the eternal advantages of the right focus:

> *So we do not look at what we can see right now, the troubles all around us, but we look forward to the joys in heaven which we have not yet seen. The troubles will soon be over, but the joys to come will last forever.*
> 2 Corinthians 4:18 (TLB)

Because we humans need immediate rewards, Paul tells us there are Earthly rewards for the correct focus:

> *But when the Holy Spirit controls our lives he will produce this kind of fruit in us: love, joy, peace, patience, kindness, goodness, faithfulness, gentleness and self-control.*
> Galatians 5: 22 (TLB)

Here on Earth we can enjoy God's peace if our focus is on Him. Do others know that you believe in God and trust in Him? Can they tell by your focus, your actions, your peace? Our profession gives us the perfect stage to share our Heavenly focus with others throughout the week.

Dear Father,
   Thank You for Your fruits of the spirit. Without them, we would surely feel lost. Help us to focus on You and Your will throughout the week as well as on Sundays.

Amen

## LAYING LIVES ASIDE

I have often wondered what some of my teachers would have done had they not been teachers. Many of them were brilliant in their subjects, and they could have been college professors or have been celebrated in their respective fields. Some of them may have sacrificed riches and prestige to teach in public schools. I can't help but wonder what they may have given up in order to teach me and my classmates.

John tells us how much we should be willing to give to others:

> We know what real love is from Christ's example
> in dying for us. And so we also ought to lay down
> our lives for our Christian brothers.
> 1 John 3:16 (TLB)

Although most of us do not lay down our physical lives for others, we often lay our professional or personal lives aside. We take time away from our families and friends in order to do our best for our students. We spend a good deal of time attending workshops, seminars and college courses to make ourselves more effective at our jobs. Much of our workday is outside of the 8:00 - 4:00 timeframe. We plan and assess on our own time because we attend to our students during the entire day.

We often give up our own pleasures, wants or desires in order to teach in public schools. Let's face it - we aren't paid what we deserve. We could be making more in sales or in some other business. God expects us to give ourselves to others. This means considering others' wants and needs before our own. As educators, we do this every day. We have chosen to follow our calling: to serve God and His children.

Dear Father,
    We thank You for Your example of selfless sacrifice. Help us to focus on Your children as we make our living sacrifice to You.
Amen

## Take Time to Play

Sometimes I think those of us in education are entirely too serious. We are called to our profession, so we are totally devoted to our teaching.
Each day we get up early, plan our day, get to school, work all day, stay late, and take work home with us. On weekends, we set aside a certain number of hours to catch up or plan ahead. We focus on our long-range goals and plan activities to help us get there. We often sacrifice other parts of our lives because of our calling. We take our jobs seriously because our children's lives are affected by everything that we do and say. The quality of our work also affects their future. The federal government, our states' legislators, our communities, our school boards and our numerous other bosses expect results and expect it now!

God gives us the answer to daily pressures through one of King David's songs:

> *Cast your burden on the Lord,*
> *And He shall sustain you;*
> *He shall never permit the righteous to be moved.*
> Psalm: 55:22 (NKJV)

We are permitted to cast our troubles to the Lord and allow Him to carry them for us! We are also assured that He will not allow us to slip or fall. If we are fully able to do this each day, there will be considerably more room in our attitudes for positive thoughts and service spirit.

To further relieve the pressure, we can take time to play. Each of us plays in his own way: sports, hobbies, reading, shopping, socializing, music, etc. Taking time to play can help us put things into perspective. Play can help us realize that there is a whole different side of ourselves that we too often ignore. Playing, in whatever form we choose, is fun!

Our children will remind us to play. I received a wake-up call one day when my daughter asked me if I was in a good mood. I told her that I was and asked her why she asked me that question. She replied, "Because you are laughing and joking with us!" I realized then that I had been taking life too serious lately. If it was an unusual event for my children to hear me laugh and play, then something needed to change!

You can also play each day on the job by laughing. There are many reasons why we should laugh. Laughing can be music to the soul. Many people believe that laughter has a healing power. Laughter is free, and it can be shared. Laughter can be planned or it can be spontaneous. Most of all, laughter can help relieve the pressures in our jobs. Laugh when you pat a child on the head and the nurse looks at you funny because she is checking him for head lice. Laugh when a child "gives you five" after wiping his nose. Laugh when the bus arrives 30 minutes late. Laugh because laughter, like play, helps us keep things in perspective.

We as Christians have the ultimate reason to be happy regardless of what the world has in store for us. As Jesus said:

> "Rejoice and be exceedingly glad, for great is your reward in heaven."
>
> Matthew 5:12 (NKJV)

Once in Heaven, we will wonder why we worried so much about trivial things here on Earth. Perhaps we should worry less and take advantage of what fun and laughter has to offer us each day.

Dear Father,

Thank You for the gift of happiness. Please help us to focus on our Earthly mission to joyfully serve others. At the same time, help us to focus on the eternal reward which You have given us.

Amen

## CAREER CRISIS OR CELEBRATION?

After we have been in the education business for a few years, we reach a check-point in our career. At this time, we must examine our motives and accomplishments. Are we working to achieve our goals and dreams, or are we merely earning a paycheck? Are we satisfying others or ourselves? Striving for specific personal goals or accomplishments leads to career satisfaction. It is this satisfaction that leads to joy in our jobs.

Are we happy and content with our life? If not, what is it we truly want to do? If we are not already doing it, what is holding us back? It is hard to strike out on one's own and try something different, but it is sometimes necessary for one's happiness. I also believe that God changes our direction by causing us to feel dissatisfied with our present situations. He speaks to us through our own discomfort. If you are unhappy with life the way it is, talk to God. He is waiting.

Jesus tells us that God already knows what we think and feel:

*Remember, your Father knows exactly what you need even before you ask Him!*

Matthew 6:8 (TLB)

We need to invite the Lord's counsel as we determine our goals and accomplishments. In order to avoid confusion or unhappiness, we should seek God's will for our lives. He directs our lives, and He has a plan for each one of us.

David sang about the importance of God's hand in our lives many years ago:

> *And let the beauty of the Lord our God be upon us, and establish the work of our hands for us.*
>
> Psalms 90:17 (NKJV)

Dear Father,

It is Your will that drives our lives. Please help us to remember to ask for Your counsel as we plan and evaluate our careers. Give us the courage we need to boldly seek Your will.

Amen

## RECIPE FOR SERVICE

Over the years I have discovered a recipe for maintaining a positive service attitude. It is not a secret recipe. We all know the ingredients, but we tend to lose them from time to time. A positive service attitude is difficult to maintain because so many forces can work against it. Rude customers, long hours, impossible demands, uncaring bosses, etc. can beat the service attitude right out of you! With a little knowledge and a lot of patience, we can keep our service attitudes going.

The ingredients of a positive service attitude are as follows:

1. Know who you are. Be secure in your service attitude. Be humble. You are proud of the fact that you serve others, but your ego is in check because there is no room for selfishness.
2. Be kind, caring, and empathetic toward everyone regardless of the situation.
3. Be thick-skinned. Be able to handle rejection, scorn, and harsh attitudes.
4. Have an intense desire to help others and to make a positive difference in their lives.

These are very difficult characteristics to maintain. However, Paul never said it would be easy:

> *Never be lazy in your work but serve the Lord enthusiastically.*
>
> Romans 12:11 (TLB)

Dear Father,

It is not easy to be service minded all of the time. Grant us the patience, perseverance and enthusiasm that we need to serve Your children well.

Amen

## CHAPTER 7

# FEBRUARY

February is the month for celebrating relationships. Valentine's Day helps us to focus on our mates. We also celebrate our relationships with the children and other adults in our lives. We must provide a role model of humility and selflessness for our children. They need to witness a true service attitude: thinking of others first and willingness to sacrifice for others.

The pace seems to slow down in February. Perhaps it is because we are looking into the future toward that ever-elusive Spring Break. We can help accelerate this pace through celebrations such as National Freedom Day, National School Counseling Week, Brotherhood/Sisterhood Week and Presidents' Day.

Standardized/End-of-Year Testing begin to loom over us as the time for testing closes in on us. Accountability is important, but it seems to overshadow our real purpose of "growing" children. Working together as a team, we can overcome the challenges of standardized testing and accountability.

Don't forget the New Year's Resolutions. God's fruits of the spirit are there for you if you are living in Him. Remember to do all within your power to shelter His children from the harmfulness of this world. Ask for God's help as you lead His children to Him.

## THE WRONG CROWD

How many times have you said this to a parent: "Your child has fallen in with the wrong crowd"? I have said these words on many occasions when good children begin to follow the wrong lead. It is imperative to redirect these children before something goes very wrong. We, as educators, know what terrific influence peers have on children. A child with good discipline and moral guidance can fall into the trap of listening to peers over their parents. It is amazing what awful things some "good" children will do or say to please their peers. We have seen some real surprising stories with some very unhappy endings.

What about us adults? Does the same principle apply to us? Can we become influenced by the wrong people? It is a fact that we become like those with whom we "hang around." I have seen some educators begin their careers with very positive attitudes; yet in a few short years, they are as negative as those with whom they chose to associate.

Often times we count on listening to others' experiences and ideas in order to decide how we think. We accept these experiences and opinions as truths and weave them into our own thoughts. We then act on these beliefs and perpetuate them, and before long they become wide-spread.

The ideals and beliefs that you are helping to spread - are they constructive or destructive? It is check-up time. Take a close look at the people you associate with at school. Are they ground-breaking, risk-taking, education supporting, customer pleasing, positive-minded child advocates?

We are told not to get wrapped up in the ways of the world:

> *Don't copy the behaviors and customs of this world, but be a new and different person with a fresh newness in all you do and think. Then you will learn from your own experience how his ways will really satisfy you.*
>
> Romans 12:2 (TLB)

What great advice this is. We are not to follow others' leads. We are to think for ourselves and make a conscious effort to be new, fresh and different. Then we will see through our own experiences how good life can really be!

Dear Father,
Thank You for making us individual thinkers. Please help us to stay positive and supportive of Your children.
Amen

## JUDGING AND CHANGING PEOPLE

Is there someone in your life that you would change if you could? To my experience, there are many people that have irritating habits or need to improve some area of their character. I have the answers to all of their problems if they would just ask! But changing people is not easy, and sometimes impossible. Believe it or not, some people do not want to change!

At school we sometimes do not work well together because of our differences. Our toleration of these differences can lead to a better understanding of others. This understanding can lead to a better acceptance of others. Once a foundation of acceptance is laid, we can move toward celebrating our differences. Once we are able to celebrate, we can then work together and draw upon one another's strengths. We count upon one another's strengths to complement our own talents and to minimize our weaknesses. This pooling of strengths is what makes our schools great!

Jesus gives us good advice about judging and changing others:

> *"Don't criticize, and then you won't be criticized. For others will treat you as you treat them. And why worry about a speck in the eye of a brother when you have a board in your own? Hypocrite! First get rid of the board. Then you can see to help your brother."*
> Matthew 7: 1-3,5 (TLB)

It is hard for us to see our own tiny flaws while the huge imperfections of others seem to jump out at us. Jesus tells us not to work on other people's flaws until we are rid of our own. For most of us, getting rid of all personal flaws could take some serious time and effort! Jesus wants us to help our brothers, but in a spirit of love - not jealousy or revenge. We tend to point out others' flaws in spite or jealousy rather than in a spirit of helping them to improve.

Think of someone that you really do not like. Now ask yourself why you don't like this person. What quality does this person have that causes you not to like him? Now examine that quality and turn it around. What is good about this quality? Reflect on this until you derive an answer. Now you will see the good that this person can bring to a relationship. For example, someone who is pushy can bring a quality of assertiveness to the group.

The bottom line is that when changes need to be made, we cannot force others to change. We only have control over what we do and how we react to what others do. If we can change our perceptions, attitudes, or actions then maybe those changes will affect others around us. We cannot control the behaviors of others, but we can be there to provide a positive role model for those who need to change their behaviors.

Dear Father,

We are far from perfect. We will strive to clean up our own lives before we start in on those around us. Help us to be there when we are needed by others. Give us the wisdom to help those who ask for our assistance.

Amen

## LAST PLACE

One of the hardest things for people to do is to ignore themselves and tend to others' needs. This is a tough concept for us in today's society. We are in the habit of seeking out what pleasures us. The media entices us to indulge ourselves in our every desire. We are encouraged to pleasure ourselves now and pay later. We are taught by society that we should look out for ourselves and strive to be number one. We are encouraged to win at whatever the cost. This type of lifestyle calls for selfishness. We must constantly search out what would be best for us. If our hearts and minds are full of ourselves and our own wants, there is not enough room for God and His will. We are told throughout the New Testament that we must leave ourselves and enter the lives of others. Only then are we free to allow Jesus fully into our lives. Only then can we be number one to the One who truly matters.

Jesus tells us what we must do:

> *"If any of you wants to be my follower,"* He told them, *"you must put aside your own pleasures and shoulder your cross, and follow me closely."*
>
> Mark 8:34 (TLB)

Jesus tells us to put aside our own pleasures. He also tells us to put away our interest in ourselves and turn our interest towards others. This is all our children ask of us. They simply want us to take an interest in their lives. They don't care about the long hours of planning, the validity of assessments, the success of new curriculum, or the accuracy of instructional methods. They simply want to know that they are important to us.

When it comes to making decisions in our lives, God has set our priorities as follows: consider God first, then all others, then ourselves. Notice that we come in a distant third. We are to consider ourselves last!

Dear Father,

Please help us to leave ourselves and enter the lives of others. Only then can we truly serve Your children. Although we are to consider ourselves last, we know that You consider us first.

Amen

## INDECISION

As educators we make hundreds of decisions each day. Most decisions are easy enough to make because information is available and the consequences are not great. However, sometimes we are faced with monumental decisions that greatly affect our present and future lives. When faced with this type of decision, what do you do? Who do you turn to?

God speaks to us a great deal in silence. He doesn't write on our walls, chalkboards, or computer screens. We have to be still to hear His voice. Many times He speaks to us through our "gut." We hear Him through our emotions and inner feelings. This voice or feeling is called by many names: The Holy Spirit, guardian angel, our conscience, etc. Regardless of what we call it, this voice is God speaking to us!

From personal experience, I can attest that I feel different when I am walking the wrong path. I know when I have made a bad decision, have a negative attitude, or have treated others wrong because I get an uncomfortable feeling inside of me. Once I make the right decision and remedy the situation, I feel better. I know this was God making me uncomfortable.

How does God speak to you? How does he show you the way and help you make the right decisions? Here are some ways for you to hear God:

1. Pray about the decision. Give God an opportunity to speak to you.
2. Listen to your inner feelings.
3. Listen to others. God sometimes speaks to us through the most unexpected people or events.
4. Take action. God will let you know if you are on the right path.

Advice was given to us a long time ago about thinking and praying too much or too long without taking action. Moses was praying about what to do about the Egyptians being in hot pursuit:

> *Then the Lord said to Moses, "Quit praying and get the people moving! Forward, march!"*
> Exodus 14:15 (TLB)

God does want us to slow down and pray to ask for his advice and help, but there are also times when he wants us to get moving! This is hard to do when we are afraid. However, King David shows his confidence that the Lord will take care of us:

> *Though I am surrounded by troubles, You will bring me safely through them ........... Your power will save me - the Lord will work out his plans for my life.*
> Psalm 138:7-8 (TLB)

It is nice to know that we have the perfect back-up when we need help with our decisions! We can always move forward in confidence that the Lord is on our side and that His power is with us.

Dear Father,
Help us to slow down and hear Your words. Then give us the courage to take action for Your children's sake.
Amen

## FREEDOM BOUND

As educators, we go to great effort to instill patriotism and an appreciation for freedom in our children. We teach about how our forefathers battled tyranny to create a new nation. We explore the history of our country by studying the lives of Americans who sought freedom as well as the events where our ancestors fought for freedom. Our quest for freedom can also be explored through art, literature and music.

"My Country, 'Tis of Thee" is a patriotic song with a great message. It basically says that our country was founded upon our fathers' faith in God and His plan for our freedom. We are truly fortunate to live in a nation that believes in freedom and equality for all people. Although our society has its flaws, most of us make a special effort to respect each other's rights and live peacefully with one another.

However, it seems that we are moving away from the ideal of grounding our society upon God's will. Human selfishness has led us to move away from God's law and toward our own ideas of freedom. As a result, the farther we move away from God, the less free we become. Without God, we must worry about violence, poverty, war, prejudice, greed, anger, and revenge - to name a few. This worry binds us in selfish fear and prevents us from thinking of others.

Paul warns us about getting too involved in the ways of the world:

> ..... *and as Christ's soldier do not let yourself become tied up in worldly affairs, for then you cannot satisfy the one who has enlisted you in His army.*
>
> 2 Timothy 2:4 (TLB)

To be truly free, we must free ourselves from Earthly matters so we can concentrate on pleasing God. With God we can be free of worry, and His peace will free us to serve others. This is the kind of freedom that we must teach our children. This is the freedom that they can count on in the long run.

Dear Father,
Help our nation to realize that only through Your law can we truly be free. Thank You for Your peace and freedom.

Amen

## TEAM-BUILDING

In professional sports, everyone has their favorite teams. Fans talk about their teams constantly and pack the stadiums to see them play. Devoted fans know how their teams are faring and support them one-hundred percent. They anticipate the opportunity to see their teams play. They celebrate their wins and despair in their defeats. Fans also have their favorite players which they admire. They talk about their favorite players and wear clothes that remind them of their heroes.

In amateur sports, we can experience these emotions for ourselves as we play together as teammates. We support each other, and together we celebrate our victories and console one another in our defeats. We form a bond with one another that is unique and powerful.

I wish educational teams were similar to sports teams. But we often don't know if we are winning or losing. We do not know for certain if our game plans are working, so we change them constantly. We aren't sure who the superstar teachers are, and we can't seem to get our fans behind us, much less get them to pack our schools!

We, as educators, can learn much in the area of team-building from the sports profession. We should envision a common goal and pursue it with a passion. We should encourage one another to do our best. We should celebrate our victories and take our defeats personally. Educators should celebrate by giving one another high fives when things are going well and encourage one another in our setbacks.

As in our physical development, we move through several stages as we grow in our professional lives. We begin as dependent people. We depend on someone to train us as we begin our profession. Then we move to independence as we see that we can make it on our own. After independence, it is crucial that we move to interdependence. At this stage we work together to produce a product better than one could produce alone. Only as a team can we serve our children to the best possible educational experience. It takes an entire school staff to create a great learning environment!

Paul tells us to think of others. We are to be a team and support each other:

> *Let nothing be done through selfish ambition or conceit, but in lowliness of mind let each esteem others better than himself. Let each of you look out not only for his own interests, but also for the interests of others.*
>
> Philippians 2: 3-4 (NKJV)

As staff members, if we act through selfish ambition or conceit, we become our own worst enemies. Looking out for the interests of others means making decisions based upon what is best for the whole school, not ourselves. It also means supporting one another and holding others' needs above our own wants. It also means watching each others' backs and picking one another up when we are down.

Let's find the team spirit in ourselves and get excited about winning.

Let's celebrate our successes and enjoy each step we take every day!

Dear Father,

It takes all of us to raise Your children according to Your will. Help us to put others first and consider ourselves last. Guide us to support one another in our efforts to best serve Your children.

Amen

## FORGIVENESS

Have you witnessed the awesome power of forgiveness? I have seen and experienced it many times myself. I have seen it change the lives of educators, students, and parents. If your life has ever been burdened by an unforgiven act, you know what I mean. Once forgiveness takes place, life is totally different. Everything looks, smells, sounds, and feels better. Life seems to have more meaning, and one feels several pounds lighter!

If you are currently in an unforgiven situation, it is easy enough to correct. You might be on either side of the issue. If you need to forgive, drop your pride and do it. If you need forgiveness, drop your pride and ask for it. If the other person is unwilling to forgive, talk to God and ask for His assistance. His wisdom and guidance supersedes our human faults.

God has advice for us on forgiveness:

> *Be gentle and ready to forgive; never hold grudges. Remember, the Lord forgave you, so you must forgive others.*
>
> Colossians 3:13 (TLB)

An important point to remember: God will not forgive us if we do not forgive others (Matthew 6:14). This is a very scary concept! We cannot expect something from God that we are unwilling to give ourselves. We must be willing to forgive. Look at it this way - forgiving is not something we do for others, it is something we do for ourselves!

Think of your school's climate. Is there an air of forgiveness? Do people hold grudges, or are they willing to forgive and forget? If not, get together and discuss the freedom which is allowed by forgiveness and push for it at your school. Forgiving is an important quality for the adults to model in our schools. Our children must learn to forgive, and they will learn best by watching us forgive one another.

Dear Father,

Forgive us where we have failed You and help us to forgive our neighbors. We need the freedom, peace and happiness that forgiveness can bring. Help us establish a forgiving atmosphere at our school.

Amen

## No Middle Ground

I remember my kindergarten teacher. She was a grandmotherly-type person who was very patient, very cuddly, and always smiling. She would often tell my mother that I was gifted with a sense of humor and that this should never be taken away from me. I cannot remember my first grade teacher at all. My mother tells me about her, but I have no recall of her whatsoever. My mother tells me that my teacher was often frustrated because I was a "clown." My teacher didn't particularly like me and had very little good to say about me.

Are there teachers in your past that you cannot remember? Are there teachers that you will remember for the rest of your life? My guess is that teachers we remember either left a very loving, positive memory in our heads or a sour taste in our mouths. The teachers we cannot remember left very little impression due to minimal personal interaction.

We educators leave either a positive or a negative impression upon our children. We work with our students 7 hours a day, 5 days a week. How can we not make some kind of an impression on their lives? Children are highly impressionable and vulnerable, and they are formulating their outlook on life while in our schools.

I believe there is no middle ground. An educator who chooses to have no personal interaction with children is choosing to leave a negative influence. It is our duty to care for all of our students and show them that they are important. It is our duty to leave a positive, lasting impression. To do anything less is a disservice to our children.

Paul tells us to take time to love each other:

> *Learn to put aside your own desires so that you will become patient and godly, gladly letting God have His way with you. This will make possible the next step, which is for you to enjoy other people and to like them, and finally you will grow to love them deeply.*
>
> 2 Peter 1:6-7 (TLB)

Jesus took the time to visit with some of the most unpopular people of His time. He was often criticized for this. He took the time to let everyone know that they were important to Him. Jesus tells us it is important to Him how we treat others:

> *"Assuredly, I say to you, inasmuch as you did it to one of the least of these My brethren, you did it to Me."*
>
> Matthew 25: 40 (NKJV)

How we interact with our children is also how we interact with Christ. This week let's take our most unlovable, undisciplined children aside and talk to them. Let's show them that we care and that they are important. All children are looking for someone who believes in them or at least cares enough to try. It may not work the first time, but persistence is the key.

Jesus also tells us often about the gift of eternal life. What a great set-up! We get to be good to one other here on Earth and experience the joy of loving and serving others. And to top it off, the reward for all of this is a blissful, eternal life with God. What a bargain!

Dear Father,

Thank You for the gift of eternal life in Heaven with You. Help us to share that news and the joy with others. Give us the wisdom to know what to say and do for those who need our attention. Help us to take the time to build a relationship with each of our students.

Amen

## CHAPTER 8

# MARCH

March is the month of the long stretch to Spring Break. Everyone is tired and this seems to override everything. Patience and forgiveness are especially important at this time of year. We must focus on the importance of tolerance and flexibility when dealing with others this month. Our students need to see us model these guiding principles. It is important to keep the proper focus - serving God and others first.

The beginning of March usually offers Public Schools Week and Open House. These activities alone are enough to keep us busy. As tired as we are, we need to celebrate our profession because we are the foundation of our society. Collectively, we determine the future of our country! Toward the end of the month, we celebrate Spring Break. This vacation rejuvenates most of us for the rest of the school year. This week we are allowed to focus on ourselves. We can relax or play hard, whichever we prefer.

Usually, the last seriously cold blast hits us in March. The first day of Spring falls in this month, and Spring-like weather seems to beckon us outside (we are often drawn outside too early and become victims of a late frost). This is a good time to praise our Lord for His beautiful Earth and the newness of life that Spring represents.

## GENTLENESS

Some people are amazed that children can approach a principal these days with a smile and a hug. "What happened to the days when students were afraid of the principal?" they want to know. They further state, "It used to be that when you saw the principal, you knew you were in big trouble." Principals once carried big paddles and spoke with loud voices. I think leadership by intimidation is on its way out, and it certainly is not my choice of leadership style. I like to speak softly, put my trust in others, and use the "big stick" only when necessary.

As educators, we are charged with keeping our emotions under control even as those around us are losing their cool. It is very difficult to remain calm while there are storms all around. We may appear to lose a confrontation when we restrain our emotions and maintain control. Some people believe that aggressive behavior and foul language will help them prevail. However, we know that the conflicts are best settled by maintaining a level head and calm demeanor.

Some people see gentleness as a sign of weakness. However, as educators, we know that it takes great strength to restrain emotion and be gentle. We are stronger than those who lose their control and lash out at others.

God tells us from where our true strength will come:

> *For thus says the Lord God, the Holy One of Israel: "In returning and rest you shall be saved; In quietness and confidence shall be your strength."*
>
> Isaiah 30:15 (NKJV)

God can give us the strength we need to remain calm. He can give us the "thick skin" we need to stay in control. We can remain confident that God will be our "big stick," and that He will give us the strength that we need to prevail.

Often, we find ourselves in the middle of conflict. We certainly do not look for trouble, but it seems to find us. Paul gives us directions to follow as we find ourselves involved in a battle of wills:

> *Avoid foolish and ignorant disputes, knowing that they generate strife. And a servant of the Lord must not quarrel but be gentle to all, able to teach, patient, in humility correcting those who are in opposition.*
> 2 Timothy 2:23-25 (NKJV)

We are told to avoid conflict. As a servant of the Lord, we are instructed to go out of our way to see that peace and harmony are maintained. This is not easy. It is often difficult to keep from saying what is on our minds (some of us have sore tongues from the constant biting). It is also made clear to us that God expects us to be humble, patient and gentle toward His children.

It is reassuring to know that God is aware of how difficult it is for us to stay calm amidst attacks. He is prepared to offer us the strength that we need to overcome our own emotions. All we need to do is go to Him and ask for His guidance and strength.

Dear Father,

Please help us to be gentle toward others. In times of confrontation, keep us calm so that we can do Your will. Help us to be patient with Your children so that we can teach them to be patient and gentle with one another.

Amen

## TEST OF FORTITUDE

One morning at school, I was verbally assaulted in the middle of the main hallway by a very angry mother. Her perception was that her children were being mistreated. As she continued to speak, she became very abusive with her language. She refused my request to carry the conversation to my office, and she continued to yell and curse there in the hallway. In a very trashy manner, she yelled out some very foul words assaulting my character and stormed out of the building.

My emotional side said to have her barred from campus and to file verbal assault charges. My professional side said to deal firmly with the situation, but to also do my best to mend the school-parent relationship. Through several phone calls and meetings, I think I successfully accomplished the latter. At least she got another chance.

On my way home that night, I asked myself (and not for the first time), "Why do I pour my heart and soul into this job only to be treated like this?" After brooding over this question for several hours, the answer hit me. I remembered that toward the end of the day a student came up to me in the hall and asked me if I was okay. I asked him what he meant by that. He said, "You know.......about this morning." Obviously, he had witnessed the event and was concerned about me. Now I remember why I put up with the pain ....... because of students like this.

God promises us that tribulations can strengthen us:

> *We also glory in tribulations, knowing that*
> *tribulation produces perseverance*
>
> Romans 5: 3 (NKJV)

It is important to note that we are told that we should not merely endure tribulations, we should glory in them! We should cheerfully face each challenge and be thankful for them. God gives us strength and allows us to transcend the problems of the world when we focus on His will for us. It is our faith in God that helps us win the daily Earthly battles. Each struggle makes us stronger and better able to carry out our mission to serve God and His children.

God also tells us that when we go through fiery trials, just like precious metals, we come out purer than ever before:

*When He has tested me, I shall come forth as gold.*
Job 23:10 (NKJV)

It is exciting to know that our daily struggles can purify us and better prepare us to serve others. I like to think that all experiences in our lives have a purpose. Our reaction to these experiences make all the difference. They can either build us up or tear us down. The decision is ours.

Dear Father,
Help us to concentrate on the joy of serving others, not the pain that sometimes comes with it. Help us to see the good in everyone and everything. Thank You for each adventure that we experience. Give us the wisdom and strength to use these experiences to make us stronger and better able to serve You.
Amen

## WHEN TO LET GO

At one time, I thought I could solve any problem that I came across. I know now that this is not true. There are situations that I cannot solve. There are children who I cannot get to behave. There are parents with whom I cannot negotiate. There are staff members whose attitudes toward children and education I cannot make more positive. There are bosses who I cannot get to listen to me.

I don't like it when a situation seems to be out of my control or influence. I don't like it when a problem cannot be solved at my level. I don't like to admit that I failed to accomplish something on my own. It takes a lot of courage for me to ask for help because it requires me to admit that I cannot do it alone.

In spite of my distaste for failure, I've decided that I can't save every child alone. Some situations are beyond my expertise. I owe it to my students to let go of my ego and seek help from others when I need it.

I know that help is available from parents, colleagues, professionals outside of public education, community members, religious leaders and God Himself.

We often forget to go to God with our problems. We exhaust all of our efforts first. Then when things are really "messed-up," we finally turn to Him with our problems. Once we go to God for His help, we accomplish our tasks with ease and go beyond our original expectations:

> *Now glory be to God who by His mighty power at work within us is able to do far more than we would ever dare to ask or even dream of - infinitely beyond our highest prayers, desires, thoughts, or hopes.*
>
> Ephesians 3:20 (TLB)

The infinite power to teach all children and to solve all problems lies within each of us. All we have to do is let go of our desire to work alone and ask God to work through us.

Dear Father,

We know that we cannot do everything by ourselves. Please remind us to call upon You for help each day. Only with Your guidance and assistance can we make a positive difference in Your children's lives.

Amen

## CAN WE TAKE IT?

"How much of this can I take?" How many times have you asked yourself this question lately? My guess is more often than you would have liked. Thinking of all of the children with poor self-discipline, the hours of grading papers, the after school meetings, and the weekends spent planning lessons is enough to make anyone consider throwing in the towel. Also, people all around us (our supervisors, other educators, students, parents, tax payers, the media and school boards) have very high expectations of us, and they can sometimes be quite abusive. With all of the long hours, hard work, thanklessness, pressures, and criticisms surrounding us, it is easy to wonder, "How much more can I take before I give up on this job?"

Paul gives good advice to those who are weary:

> *And let us not grow weary while doing good, for in due season we shall reap if we do not lose heart.*
> 
> Galatians 6:9 (NKJV)

We are told not to grow weary or to lose heart because in the long-run we will reap the benefits for doing good things here on Earth. This is sound advice, but it is difficult to implement because we like to receive immediate rewards for what we do. Often times, our immediate pressures and troubles do not quickly melt away simply because we try to concentrate on eternal rewards.

It is going to take more than a hot bath to make some of our headaches go away. I challenge you to take a hard look at yourself and your students. Ask yourself, "Is my presence here enriching these students' lives?" Once you have honestly answered this question, you are ready to examine your options. If you choose to stay in education, you will want to seek the endurance that you will need to keep serving God's children and to maintain a positive state of mind.

We can discover the endurance that we need if we keep up our courage and maintain our joy and trust in the Lord:

> *Christ, God's faithful son, is in complete charge of God's house. And we Christians are God's house - He lives in us! - if we keep up our courage firm to the end, and our joy and our trust in the Lord.*
> 
> Hebrews 3:6 (TLB)

Our prize for trusting in God is joy. Joy is not a come and go emotion like happiness. Joy is the firm foundation laid through faith in God and in His plan for our lives. Joy is the security of knowing that God is with us every minute of every day. Joy is knowing that we are unconditionally loved and celebrated by God throughout our Earthly life and our everlasting life. With rewards like these, we should be able to endure our trials and tribulations one hundred fold!

We need to remind one another of the joy and strength that God has to offer us. Let's remember to do this daily!

Dear Father,

Help us not to become weary as we try to accomplish Your will. Please renew us by rekindling our joy of serving others. We will trust in You to give us the endurance we need to face our daily challenges.

Amen

## How Great Art Thou?

Have you ever asked yourself, "How good am I?" In today's competitive world, this is a very valid question. As we struggle to do our best, it is only natural to want to compare ourselves to others. Many of us compete with each other as we climb the corporate ladder or look for the success that will elevate us above the rest. We are often competitive as we work together. We like to see our students create the best projects, perform the best on standardized tests, and be the best behaved throughout the school. Some of us like to compete for educator awards and receive recognition for our accomplishments. We tend to equate our job success with our self-worth. Unfortunately, it is when we begin to congratulate ourselves for our accomplishments that we begin to fail.

Success can be one of the greatest dangers we face in life. Praise from our fellow man can also be dangerous. It can lead us to think too much of ourselves. Success here on Earth can separate us from God. As we trust more in ourselves, our jobs, our families, our homes, or our material possessions, we trust less in God. The more we focus on ourselves and our own achievements, the less we think of God and His purpose for our lives.

We are told that God searches our hearts for our true motives:

*He searches all hearts and examines deepest motives so*
*He can give to each person his right reward, according to*
*his deeds - how he has lived.*
Jeremiah 17:10 (TLB)

We should examine what it is that drives us. Is it a desire to be admired by others, or is it to give our best to God's children so that they will prosper? God knows, and He is preparing our reward in accordance to our motives and our deeds!

Dear Father,
Thank You for giving us the desire to be the best. Help us balance our desire to be the best with our desire to do our best for Your children.
Amen

## ONE GOOD FRIDAY

One Good Friday
not very long ago,
our world as we know it
hit its lowest low.

We showed our most human traits
fear, jealousy, envy and deceit,
as we took God's greatest gift
and trampled Him under our feet.

Because we did not understand
we demanded death in God's name.
So Jesus walked to His crucifixion
thus adding to our shame.

The world spent the next day and darkest night
with no more hope for future light.

The third day, God again proved His love
with one more miracle for us to see.
He collected up all of our ugly sins
and set each one of us free.

The one we murdered was not man alone
His victory - an opened grave,
for He is Jesus, Son of God, King of Kings
His mission - our lives to save.

Today His resurrection gives us hope,
prayers to pray and songs to sing.
Because of Jesus' sacrifice and God's grace
we now have life everlasting.

> *"For God so loved the world that He gave his only begotten Son, that whoever believes in Him should not perish but have everlasting life."*
>
> John 3:16

Dear Father,
   Thank You for the gift of eternal life through Your Son's supreme sacrifice. Help us to slow down and meditate on Your love and grace during this Holy Week.

Amen

## TRUTH OR DARE

Truth or Dare is a game where you either tell the truth to the group or you accept a dare to do in the place of the truth. Often you find taking the dare leads to a significantly embarrassing consequence. In other words, you decide how important it is to you to avoid telling the truth.

We play truth or dare all of the time. We often avoid telling the truth to parents. They sometimes are not prepared to hear the painful truth about their children's academic or behavioral progress. They get mad and communications and relationships break down. We often hold back our feelings with children in order to maintain their self-esteem. We are often dishonest with colleagues in order to spare feelings and preserve relationships. In other words, we can get pretty good at lying to one another!

I am not sure that we have to lie to each other to get along. Relationships based upon deceit and half-truths do not exist on solid foundations. We are told that the Holy Spirit will help us to peacefully exist with one another:

> *Try always to be led along together by the Holy Spirit, and so be at peace with one another.*
>
> Ephesians 4:3 (TLB)

If we follow the guidance of the Holy Spirit, we can build our interpersonal relationships on solid ground. Some examples of building blocks for good relationships are:

1. honest, careful, constructive feedback to one another
2. acceptance of differences - physical, intellectual, philosophical, emotional, and spiritual
3. protection of one another and mutual trust
4. openness to new ideas and opinions
5. unconditional love

Dear Father,

Thank You for the honesty in our relationships. Help us to be honest and trusting with one another.

Amen

## Go With It

Sometimes the greatest lessons are the least planned ones. I remember one day I exchanged places with a student in the classroom. He was a very difficult student to teach. He was always interrupting and wise-cracking from his seat. I constantly had to redirect him back on- task. One day I had enough. After numerous interruptions, I asked him if he would like to teach the class. He laughed and said that he would. He got up and started clowning as the teacher.

Then an idea hit me. I took his place in the audience and began wise-cracking! I had the best time watching him squirm. The students thought it was hilarious. Everyone had a good time, and we all learned something from it. I think we all walked out of that room respecting one another's position more. I realize now that I must have appeared "a bit nutty" to the students, but I think this episode made me a little more human to the students.

Spontaneity is enjoying each moment for what it has to offer. We should make an effort to enjoy our journey in life even if it means deviating from the planned path. Sadly, even though we spend countless hours planning our lessons to the most minute details, it may be those special spontaneous, "off the wall" moments that the students remember the most.

A song in the book of Habakkuk speaks to us about enjoying the journey:

> *Yet I will rejoice in the Lord, I will joy in the God of my salvation. The Lord is my strength; He will make my feet like deer's feet, And He will make me walk on my high hills.*
>
> Habakkuk 3:18-19 (NKJV)

At work, home, or in between, we can rejoice in the Lord, and he will help us to walk on the clouds. We can enjoy every minute of our journey if we walk with the Lord.

Dear Father,

Please help us to be more spontaneous and enjoy each minute for what it has to offer. Help us to make the most of them and use them to Your children's benefit.

Amen

## CHAPTER 9

# APRIL

April is a busy month. It usually includes standardized testing, proms, banquets, sports tournaments, field trips, etc. Celebrations such as Keep America Beautiful Month, Mathematics Education Month, National Library Week, National Volunteer Week, Professional Secretaries' Week, Week of the Young Child, Take Our Daughters to Work Day and National Arbor Day give us ideas for exciting activities for our students.

This month the last grading period begins, and we are facing our last chance to help students achieve success. We often feel extreme pressure at this point to get our students to meet state standards. Teamwork can pull our school through the fires of standardized testing. Remember, it is who you've got, not what you've got, that makes the difference. It is our teachers, not our materials or programs, that truly determine our students' success.

The month of April is packed with activities, yet it seems to pass by slowly. For many of us this month begins the longest stretch of the year, from April Fool's Day to the last day of school. Unfortunately, the weather at this time of year is not cooperative. It is quite rainy and gloomy most of the time, and we find ourselves rarely getting outside to expend our excess energy.

April is a dangerous month for relationships. With the year coming to a close too quickly and frustrations flaring all around us, we need to model and practice patience and empathy. Our fortitude is tested by every negative circumstance. Ask God for His strength and protection. Work with Him on forgiving others as well as yourself.

This can be the most challenging month for student discipline. Perhaps the best defense is a good offense. Plenty of activities to keep everyone busy and out of trouble might be the key. This calls for extensive planning up front, but it pays huge dividends. Work together with your colleagues to determine the most effective activities for your students.

## STANDARDIZED TESTS/ NONSTANDARDIZED CHILDREN

One of the greatest frustrations for educators today is the loss of freedom in teaching due to standardized testing. We feel smothered by the expectations put upon us by outside forces. And often it is questionable whether these forces truly know what is the best education for children. In the classrooms, we can see the adverse results of too much pressure on children to succeed. We often force children to learn at a level that is too advanced or at a pace that is too fast. We force nonstandardized pegs into a standardized hole. Imagine us physically poking and shoving children into a holes that are not big enough for them. It would be a painful experience for students and teachers alike. How close is reality to this image? We educators already feel that we are sometimes expected to do the impossible at a terrible cost to the children.

We are under a lot of pressure to increase standardized test scores. I prefer to think of it as pressure to increase students' learning. We should always pressure ourselves to increase our effectiveness in helping children learn. Curriculum or materials alone will not make the difference for our children. The greatest factor is the personal relationship established between the child and the teacher who is dedicated to helping that individual child succeed. The best teachers are those who are informed and flexible. These teachers are driven to do whatever it takes to ensure a student's success. They will use whatever curriculum or materials they think works best for their students; picking the best parts from many different systems, putting their own touches to them and adding them to their own teaching repertoires. If we keep our focus on the children and do what is best for them, we will continue to cover essential skills and the standardized tests will take care of themselves.

We are given advice on what is most important in life:

*In response to all he has done for us, let us outdo each other in being helpful and kind to each other and in doing good.*

Hebrews 10:24 (TLB)

We owe it to our Lord to try to outdo each other in kindness and goodness toward others. We must establish relationships with our children based upon love and kindness. We must consider each child's needs as we determine what to teach. Our children are not standardized; therefore our approach to loving and teaching them should not be standardized.

Dear Father,
Thank You for not standardizing us. We glory in our individuality. Help us to treat Your children differently according to their own needs.

Amen

## MEDITATIONS

Katharine Hepburn once said "Listen to the song of Life." Can you think of a more beautiful way to say, "Stop and smell the roses?" In the hustle and bustle of life, we often forget to do this. Think of the beautiful music we miss because we are in a hurry! As followers of God, we are promised the ability to experience compassion, kindness, humility, gentleness, patience, forgiveness, love, and peace. However, we diminish our ability to enjoy these fruits of the spirit as we hurry through our rapid-paced lives. Think of a typical day at school. How many fruits of the spirit do you experience? Perhaps we are losing out on these blessings from God. So how can we recapture these gifts?

First of all, we can get out of our ruts by not always doing the same things. We can look for something new and fun to do. We can get in touch with the child in us and let our guard down. We can do something crazy and surprise everyone. Spontaneity and variety are the spice of life!

Second, we can avoid dwelling on the negative. We can make ourselves see the positive side of things (no matter how long and hard we have to look). We can be aware of the good in life and spend less time contemplating the bad - especially those people and events in which we have no control.

The last suggestion is the most important. We must slow down and find the time to meditate. This will involve rearranging or changing our priorities. God is always with us, but we don't hear Him unless we are quiet. Only then can we hear what He has to say to us. By allowing Him to speak to us and guide us, we will see that through Him we can overcome the world.

Paul gives us great advice about how to think:

> *Finally, brethren, whatever things are true, whatever things are noble, whatever things are just, whatever things are pure, whatever things are lovely, whatever things are of good report, if there is any virtue and if there is anything praiseworthy - meditate on these things. The things which you learned and received and heard and saw in me, these do, and the God of peace will be with you.*
>
> Philippians 4: 8-9 (NKJV)

We are promised God's peace if we will meditate on that which is good. It is not easy because we tend to focus on the negative. We need to make a conscious effort to slow down, count our blessings and appreciate all that is good in life!

Dear Father,

Please help us keep our minds on You and Your will. With Your help, we can concentrate on the good in those around us - especially Your children. Help us to dwell on the positive events in our lives and to leave the pitfalls in Your hands.

Amen

## HIDE AND SEEK

Children have a game that they have played for generations called Hide and Seek. There are now many variations on the game, but essentially it consists of one person seeking another until the other is found. The game can last seconds or hours depending on the rules. Think back to when you played the game. What was the thrill for you? Was it the process of seeking others and being surprised when you found them or was it the process of hiding and springing out at someone when they found you? Maybe it was showing off your prowess as you detected where the others hid or by finding the perfect hiding spot that no one else could find.

We still play Hide and Seek every day as adults. As educators, we constantly seek knowledge and success. We seek the perfect math system, the perfect reading program, the perfect discipline model, the perfect diagnostic or evaluation tool, etc. Being adverse to failure like we are, we seek these answers with the same desperation that we showed when we searched for friends years ago in a game. Have you found all of the answers to your educational challenges: curriculum, instruction, discipline, evaluation, and time management? Have you found all of the answers for the challenges in your personal life? If not, where do you go from here?

Jesus has an answer for us:

> *"Ask, and it will be given to you; seek and you will find; knock, and it will be opened to you. For everyone who asks*

*receives, and he who seeks finds, and to him who knocks it will be opened."*

Matthew 7:7-8 (NKJV)

Too often we depend only upon our own resources in searching for answers. We wait until we have exhausted all other avenues before we, in frustration, go to God. Jesus tells us to seek our answers through God's will. It sure sounds like a time-saver!

Dear Father,
Please help us to remember that we are not alone. You have the answers that we seek. Thank You for allowing us to come to You for solutions.

Amen

## LET GO AND LET GOD

I have heard the popular saying "Let go and let God" many times. It tells me to go to God more often and not be so independent. It tells me that worrying about situations isn't nearly as effective as turning them over to God. It is a reminder that we are not in this life by ourselves. This is a great saying, but it is very hard advice to follow.

We constantly struggle to include God more in our personal lives; however we often leave God out of our professional lives. We forget that He does not leave us on Monday mornings and return to us on Friday evenings. God is on call around the clock seven days a week - even at school. He doesn't believe in separation of church and state (we did that to ourselves)!

We spend a lot of time planning in our jobs. We create daily lesson plans, weekly plans, semester plans, and yearly plans. We plan time lines for our curriculum so that we accomplish all of our goals in a year's time. We plan extra curricular activities and classroom management procedures. Once all of this is done, we implement our plans and hope that they are successful.

Perhaps we should rely less upon ourselves and spend more time planning with God. Here are three major areas of our professional lives in which we can rely more upon God:

1. Student Discipline

We can ask God to help us open our hearts to our children. We can show the love of God by developing a caring relationship with each child, yet firmly teaching them right from wrong. God will give us the wisdom and patience we need to steer our children toward His will.

2. Innovative/Creative Strategies

We can ask God to open our minds to new possibilities and trust that He will inspire us and give us the ideas that we need to motivate our children. We can ask for help with our many decisions on how to best instruct our students. God can help us decide just what the children need.

3. Interpersonal Relationships

We can ask God to help us be patient with one another (students and fellow educators) and treat everyone with dignity and respect. All of us need help with this. Only through strong interpersonal relationships can we help others grow.

We have been given the ultimate advice about planning:

> *Don't worry about anything; instead, pray about everything; tell God your needs and don't forget to thank Him for His answers.*
>
> Philippians 4:6 (TLB)

We are told to include God in everything we do. Notice that we are not told to try everything we can think of first and then call on God. For true success, we are to call on Him for everything. We are also told to check in with a "thank you" when He helps us! Can we afford to pass up a consultant who has proven to be 100% accurate in all decisions?

Dear Father,

Thank You for Your constant presence. Help us to be aware of Your presence and count on You for help in our daily lives.

Amen

## ONE DAY AT A TIME

Have you noticed how educators tend to think in the future? Together, we are always planning long-range and short-range goals, projects, and special events for our schools. Individually, we each plan ahead for lessons, units, and assessments. We also quite often find ourselves reflecting on and learning from the past. With all of this time spent learning from the past and looking ahead to the future, how much time do we really spend enjoying the present?

What prevents us from enjoying the present? Regrets of the past often rob us from enjoying today. We do not forgive the transgressions of the previous day and begin anew, thus allowing guilt to cloud our pleasure. Fear of the future can also take away the joy of the present. Dreading tomorrow, next week, or next month can hide the joys of today.

Regret or fear can cause us to miss-out on the present, but often the problem is simply forgetting to slow down and appreciate the every- day events. The function of the modern day poet is to slow down, observe life, get in touch with the human spirit, and report findings back to others. Perhaps each of us should get in touch with the poet within us.

Missed opportunities are great tragedies. We must live for today because it is all we are guaranteed. We should be aware of God's beautiful Earth. There is so much to observe and be grateful for.

God and Jesus tell us the time to experience joy is now:

> *"So don't be anxious about tomorrow. God will take care of your tomorrow too. Live one day at a time."*
> Matthew 6:34 (TLB)

> *This is the day the Lord has made; We will rejoice and be glad in it!*
> Psalms 118:24 (NKJV)

Dear Father,

    Thank you for creating this beautiful world for us. Help us to slow down and take advantage of what this world has to offer each day we are here.

Amen

## SECRETARIES' DAY

A Special love poem to our Secretaries who:

Can carry on multi-conversations and tasks
and answer our questions even before we ask.

Can please all staff, no matter how picky;
will clean up others' messes, no matter how icky.

Often accept blame for what others do
and refuse compliments, regardless how few.

Are always willing to serve up dignity by the bowl-full
even to those who act like a whole-fool.

Will take bullets meant for another,
hand out reminders even better than a mother.

Can pull us out of any scrape
with only glue, white-out, scissors or tape.

Most of all we appreciate that loyal smile
that allows us to postpone our troubles for a while.

Because we are thankful for their presence each day,
we ask God for a very special blessing to come their way.

Happy Secretaries' Day

Secretaries are our unsung heroes in education. They are fiercely loyal, incredibly hard-working, and great public relations agents for our schools. They are over-worked, under-paid, under-appreciated and taken for granted. However, they continue to smile and support us each day.

Our secretaries are way ahead of most of us when it comes to sacrifice. They shoulder much more of the burden than is required of them. They truly are following Christ's law:

> *Bear one another's burdens, and so fulfill the law of Christ.*
>
> Galatians 6:2 (NKJV)

Dear Father,
Thank You for our loyal secretaries who shoulder our burdens every day. Help us to better show our appreciation for their support.
Amen

## DUMP THE MENTAL GARBAGE

Have you noticed how a garbage can smells after a couple of days if you miss the regular garbage pick-up? It fouls the air and overwhelms your senses. This is exactly what happens if "mental garbage" lies around in your brain for very long. It can begin to foul your mind and take over your positive thoughts. Mental garbage is made up of resentment, jealousy, revenge, pessimism, as well as any other negative thoughts. These are very powerful human emotions, and they occur within each of us. These emotions are dangerous to us because as they lie around and fester, they can pollute our minds and foul every aspect of our lives.

Rumor and gossip are the vehicles in which this mental garbage can be spread. Every workplace has its best breeding spot for this mental garbage to grow and do its damage. Where is this spot in your school? Is it the staff lounge? the office? the parking lot? Is the rumor mill alive and well at your school? Are you a vital link in the gossip chain?

God tells us through King Solomon that rumors and lies are very powerful weapons:

> *A man who bears false witness against his neighbor*
> *is like a club, a sword, and a sharp arrow.*
>
> Proverbs 25: 18 (NKJV)

We must dump these powerful weapons before they hurt someone and cause irreparable damage to the climate of the school. Not only do we need to drop the weapons of gossip and rumors, but we need to cleanse our minds of the smelly mental garbage that arms these weapons.

Once we rid our minds of mental garbage, we are directed to replace it with kindness:

> *Since you have been chosen by God who has given you*
> *this new kind of life, and because of His deep love and*
> *concern for you, you should practice tenderhearted mercy*
> *and kindness to others.*
>
> Colossians 3:12 (TLB)

Dumping mental garbage is difficult because society tends to steer us toward negative thoughts. All you have to do is tune into prime time television or read a newspaper to get the latest in pessimism and negativism. We can learn to recognize negative thoughts and consciously rid ourselves of them, but being positive requires a sustained, purposeful effort on our part. We must make a conscious effort every day to keep our thoughts positive.

It will help to find those people in your school that steer clear of the negative. Converse with them daily. They will help by encouraging you to think positively. By seeking out these positive people, you will also avoid those who are mired in their own dark, self-defeating attitudes. Beware of these people. They will seek you out because they seek to add your company to their misery. Disappoint them by being a role model of positive thinking. They need to see what a positive attitude can do for them.

Dear Father,
Help us to cleanse our minds of all mental garbage and refill them with Your mercy and kindness. Please keep our minds focused on Your love and inspire us with ideas of how to accomplish Your will.

Amen

## TO BE OR NOT TO BE

In the classroom we are constantly "on stage." Our students watch us every minute of every day. We find ourselves acting out certain roles and putting on different faces for different situations. We develop many different personalities: one for the classroom, one with professional colleagues, one for the boss, one with friends, one for home, one for church, and one for the community. We can sometimes get lost in our different roles, and we have to ask ourselves, "Which one is the real me?"

It is easy to confuse roles in different situations. We find ourselves correcting children's behavior in supermarkets, movie theaters, football games, etc. (much to the dismay of their mothers). We find ourselves straightening books or cans in stores. There are times we say "I hope none of my kids are around" when we are in public. We sometimes say or do something at school that we normally reserve for close friends or family. We have all confused our different roles at times, and it can be quite embarrassing!

It is important not to get too confused and lose our "real" selves in all the different roles that we play because we model our values and character to our children each day. We need to be sure that we are demonstrating the character that God would have us model for His children.

As Paul tells us:

> *Be their ideal; let them follow the way you teach and live; be a pattern for them in your love, your faith, and your clean thoughts.*
>
> 1 Timothy 4:12 (TLB)

We are to establish an ideal pattern for our children to follow. We are told to "walk our talk." Not only are we to have high expectations for the students' behavior, we are to exhibit an exemplary character to the students on a daily basis. What we portray "on stage" as well as in other areas of our lives should be the life that God expects us to live. It is too dangerous to live by more than one moral code because we will eventually confuse our roles and send our children the wrong message. God tells us to live by only one set of standards - His code of conduct!

With character education catching on in the public schools across the nation, educators are now being tasked to teach citizenship and moral character to the children. We can no longer concentrate mostly on academics. Our nation's moral fiber is continuing to unravel, and the public schools are being charged to reweave our moral tapestry. We need to be sure that we are modeling and teaching the character traits that will put our nation back on the right track.

Dear Father,

We will strive to live our lives by Your moral standards. Help us to be the ideal for our students and to model Your code of conduct at all times. By training Your children in Your will, we will strengthen our nation's morality.

Amen

## LIFE'S ADVENTURES

Isn't it refreshing to know that life is full of adventures? We never really know what is around the next corner..... will our next experience be of major or minor importance? Will it be depressing or exhilarating? Will it help us grow or tear us down? Each day holds the potential for ecstasy or disaster. When we wake up, we don't know which one it might be. Maybe we can't control what happens to us, but we can control how situations affect us. We can look at each experience, good or bad, as something from which to learn and grow. Each adventure has a purpose - to mold us and make us who we are.

Often our first reaction after a bad experience is to say, "Wow, I want to forget that this ever happened." This evasive action will not help us to grow. Reflecting after each experience is important. This allows us to think about what has happened and to learn from it. This is what can turn a terrible experience into a valuable one.

For example, I learned how not to teach from one of my college professors. He was a negative, cynical, hateful man who did not enjoy the company of his students. Each hour with him was a test of my fortitude. I decided to study his mannerisms to ensure that I would never exhibit those traits as a teacher. I learned a lot about how to treat others through his bad example.

We learn from everything that happens to us - successes as well as failures. Next time something adverse happens to us, we can reflect on it until we receive some form of value from it (be patient because it might take some time). There is something of value to be learned daily from every experience.

We are told that our outlook on life is dependent upon our inner-selves:

*A person who is pure of heart sees goodness and purity in everything; but a person whose own heart is evil and untrusting finds evil in everything*

Titus 1:15 (TLB)

Our outlook on life determines how we are affected by what happens to us. We can either see experiences as destructive or as growth opportunities. We can either quit or become more determined to succeed. Think of the people you know who always see the good in every situation. Now think of the people who always see the negative side. Who tends to be happier? Which outlook do you usually take?

God will help us to be pure of heart. He will help us look for the good in everything.

Dear Father,

Help us to see the good in everything that happens to us. Enable us to learn from all of our experiences and pass this knowledge on to Your children.

Amen

## CHAPTER 10

# MAY

May is a month for celebration. We celebrate graduations, promotions, academic accomplishments and end-of-year activities. "Moving forward" seems to be the motif for this month. Also, National PTA Teacher Appreciation Week and National Family Week give us reasons to celebrate important people in our lives.

May takes on a hectic pace; however the anticipation of the end of the year seems to counteract this stress. The light at the end of the tunnel seems to keep us going. We need to slow down and savor the moments we have with our colleagues and students because some of these people will be moving out of our lives. Ending some of our relationships can be painful, so ask God to help you slow down and enjoy each moment with students, friends and family.

Beautiful Spring weather and flowers seem to lend a certain air to this season. We can be thankful to God for our lives and loves here on Earth. Meditation on God and His glory can help us to appreciate our fleeting moments here on Earth and look forward to eternal life in Heaven. At the end of this month, Memorial Day gives us an opportunity to appreciate the military personnel who gave up their lives so that we can be free.

## DUMBER WORDS WERE NEVER SPOKEN

Do you know what makes me angry? That old saying: "Those who can, do. Those who can't, teach." Who made up this not-so-wise saying? It makes teachers sound like some real losers. It is true that anyone can teach. In fact all of us teach something to someone from time to time. However, the art of teaching is not a task for losers. Mastering the art of teaching is difficult. First, we must assess what the students know. Then we determine what they need to learn and how each one learns best. We make each learning experience interesting and relevant to their lives. We must then make the students understand why learning is important and motivate them to want to learn all they can and do their best. In addition to all of this, teachers are called upon to act as counselors, judges, entertainers, stage directors, negotiators, politicians, etc. Sound easy? Maybe we should let our critics take a shot at it!

We educators are victims of criticism and sarcasm from others; however we are the bedrock of our society. We are not the flashy heroes or superstars that the children most admire, but we are the solid rock that they depend upon. We may not be regarded as celebrities by society, but we are the ones that keep our country moving forward. Educators deserve the accolades and the cheers. Society should put them up on a pedestal for what they do! We should see educators on magazine covers, trading cards, and television commercials!

However, we are told that our deeds are not to be done for the public's admiration:

> *Take Care! Don't do your good deeds publicly, to be admired, for then you will lose the reward from your Father in heaven.*
>
> Matthew 6:1 (TLB)

We are not seeking to be admired or applauded. If we did, our focus would be on ourselves, not on God and His children. We are working for our Father in Heaven. He promises us that our reward is waiting for us.

Once in Heaven, we will most likely wonder why we were more concerned about Earthly praise than we were about pleasing God. We will understand that accolades from anyone other than God are trivial.

Dear Father,

We thank You for the privilege of serving You and Your children. We know that our reward is eternal life with You. Our work here is important, but it is not often recognized as such. Help us to weather the criticisms and give us the strength to do our best.

Amen

## Are You Famous?

"Mr. Stephen, are you famous?" These words floated up to me from the innocent little face of a child whose hand I was shaking. As the newly appointed assistant principal, I was walking the halls of my school, shaking hands and introducing myself to the students. I was feeling quite "pumped-up" and important at the time. Taken aback by the question, I had to think a moment. Yes, I was quite important here at this school, but hardly famous. So my answer was, "Well, I suppose I am pretty important here at this school, but I'm not famous." The more I think of my response, the less I think of it.

As educators, are we famous? I think so. By definition, famous means "having a widespread reputation; renowned; celebrated." A few educators achieve national or international acclaim. Their deeds and accomplishments are highlighted and celebrated. Those of us who don't achieve this status, still make a difference in our own communities. Perhaps millions of people do not know or admire us, but I dare say each of us affects hundreds if not thousands of lives over the span of our careers. As each year passes, more students fall under our guidance and leadership. As a result, our influence becomes more and more widespread.

It is tragic to me that many educators say to themselves and others, "I am only a teacher; only a teacher's aide; only a secretary, etc." What has happened to us? Teaching, once the noblest of professions, has lost its prestige. Because educators are not highly paid, highly publicized, or highly revered by the public, many believe the profession has lost its importance. I disagree. Educators have the most important and challenging function in our society - to shape children's lives and create the future of our world. What other profession or vocation is more crucial than this?

Be assured that we educators are highly renowned and celebrated by God. He knows of our trials and joys. He follows each of our lives day by day. He is aware of our every move. He even knows how many hairs each of us has on our heads (Matthew 10:30). We may not be famous celebrities here on Earth; but when the time is right, God will see to our reward.

The time we spend here on Earth is not to be used for storing up Earthly treasures and striving for human accolades. There is much more valuable work to be done. As Jesus said:

> *"Don't store up treasures here on earth where they can erode away or may be stolen. Store them in heaven where they will never lose their value, and are safe from thieves. If your profits are in heaven your heart will be there too."*
> Matthew 6:19-21 (TLB)

Even though society sometimes chooses to look down upon the teaching profession as ineffective and educators as "second-class" professionals, our reward is in God's hands. And His hands are the ones that make all the difference!

Dear Father,

Thank You for the opportunity we have to shape our children's lives. It is an awesome task to shape tomorrow's world, but with Your help we can do it. Guide us as we humbly serve Your children.

Amen

## SILLY SMILES

What I liked best about the Summer Olympics of 1996 were the "silly smiles" on the faces of the medallists. As they stood on the gold, silver and bronze podiums receiving their medals, they were about to explode from happiness and fulfillment. It showed on their faces, in their smiles (the kind that you just can't wipe off of your face). Have you ever been so happy that you just couldn't help but smile? Think of that time. You were so happy that you thought your heart would burst or your face would crack from that huge grin. You tried to wipe that grin off your face, but you just couldn't do it?

Next question: was this time at work? Your answer is probably, "No, of course not! Things this great do not happen at my work." I wonder why not? Some people get paid to do what they would do for free anyway. How fortunate they are! The reality is that most of us work for our pay and the silly smiles come later during our off-duty hours. I wonder if it has to be that way - especially in our line of work. Can we come up with activities with our children that will give us enough happiness and fulfillment to experience those silly smiles?

What can we do to ensure a silly smile for ourselves at work? What can we do to ensure silly smiles for others around us?

Paul makes it clear to us how we should feel every day:

*Rejoice in the Lord always. Again I will say, rejoice!*
Philippians 4:4 (NKJV)

God tells us to wear joy on our faces all of the time. He tells us to wear those silly smiles! We need to strive for those feelings of exhilaration where we feel so close to God that our whole body tingles. These fleeting moments are a sample of how Heaven will feel. So how can we ensure these silly smiles? Remember this: if our hearts are about to explode with the joy of God, how can we keep from smiling?

Dear Father,

Thank You for those moments that give us those silly smiles. Help us to multiply those moments and experience them more each day. We will share these moments with Your children.

Amen

## TAKE A NUMBER PLEASE

We often restrict our effectiveness with our customers by strictly adhering to our policies and procedures. Here is an example:

At the Municipal Court Building in the city where I live, I went to pay a traffic citation (for a friend of course). Upon entering the empty reception area, I walked up to the counter, caught the eye of one of the two receptionists and explained my mission. She asked, "Did you take a number?" Baffled, I told her that I hadn't. She pointed and said, "Take a number please. Someone will be with you shortly." I walked over to the area that she pointed to and found a ticket dispenser with a sign that instructed visitors to take a number and sit down. I took the number 20 and sat down (I had ample choice since all of the seats were empty). After about two minutes of appropriate paper shuffling, the lady said, "Sir, I can help you now." I thought about asking her to call my number, but I decided not to push my luck (I know that I have seen this before in some comedy routine).

As she processed my payment, I found myself leaning with both elbows on the counter. I then noticed at my right elbow a sign that had been taped to the counter that read: "Please do not lean on or bend over the counter." I snapped to attention and nervously waited for her to finish. At this point I just wanted out of there before I did anything else wrong. I hope I never have to go back to that place again!

Now I can't help but wonder if there are any rules or regulations at our schools that we adhere to just for the sake of following rules. If so, this is not a customer-friendly habit. Perhaps from now on, when faced with a situation where a rule doesn't seem to fit, we will seriously question the validity of that rule. We should ask of ourselves: "Are we treating our customers right?"

Paul tells us how to serve others:

> *For, dear brothers, you have been given freedom: not freedom to do wrong, but freedom to love and serve each other.*
>
> Galatians 5:13 (TLB)

We are told that we have freedom only within the boundaries of loving and serving one another. Our guidelines are to serve one another with love. When serving others out of love, we must be flexible and consider the individual circumstances of each situation. This will prevent us from possibly damaging relationships through strict adherence to rules and regulations that really don't matter anyway.

Dear Father,
   Help us to consider the needs of people over the need to follow rules and regulations. Remind us that Your children are our first priority.

Amen

## MOTHER'S DAY

Mother
Why do I love you?
Let me count the ways:

> One - because you make my life lots of fun
> Two - because you love me no matter what I do
> Three - because you chauffeur me all over the county
> Four - because you take care of my every hurt and sore
> Five - because you make me feel important and glad to be alive

Six - because you put up with my silly tricks
Seven - because you teach me about God, Jesus and Heaven
Eight - because you make me eat everything on my plate (NOT!)
Nine - because you always look so fine
Ten - because you give me hugs and kisses again and again

HAPPY MOTHER'S DAY

As we honor our mothers on this Mother's Day holiday, let's remember what God told us thousands of years ago:

> *Honor your father and your mother, that your days may be long upon the land which the Lord your God is giving you.*
>
> Exodus 20:12 (NKJV)

Mothers are perhaps the greatest of God's Earthly gifts. Their clear demonstrations of unconditional love are models for us as educators. We are to be "mothers" to our students as we display God's love to His children. God tells us we will be rewarded for our honoring of our mothers.

Dear Father,
Thank You for mothers. Help us to learn from their loving examples. We promise to "mother" Your children and teach them of Your love.

Amen

## MOVING UP

When moving up in the world the old adage often rings true: "It's not what you know it's who you know." Isn't this true? I can think of many examples illustrating the possibility that someone moved up or was recognized due to personal connections rather than superior knowledge or ability, natural talent, or hard work. I don't need to tell you that this can be very frustrating. I am not sure anyone has figured out a fair way to recognize the best educators through a meaningful compensatory or advancement system. It seems like everyone is regarded the same even though we are all different. Many times it is those who get in good with the "system" that are recognized or rewarded whether they deserve it or not.

Paul also tells us that truly it is who you know that makes the difference:

*I can do all things through Christ who strengthens me.*
Philippians 4:13 (NKJV)

There is no doubt that a personal relationship with Christ will allow us to do all things - even moving up in the professional world.

Also, when moving up in the spiritual world, it's not what you know, but who you know that makes you successful. All of the knowledge, skills, or personal connections in the world will not gain us admittance into Heaven. Only a personal relationship with God and Jesus will accomplish that. Even though we do not deserve the heavenly reward that we receive, we still move up based upon who we know.

Dear Father,
Thank You for being the only one we truly need to know in order to move up. Help us to concentrate on Heavenly rewards rather than Earthly ones.
Amen

## SERVE WHOLE-HEARTEDLY

Who cares if you work hard? Who notices that you spend late nights preparing lessons or grading papers? Who notices that you spend long afternoons at the media center or many hours decorating your room? Who notices when you deliver an outstanding lesson or finally get that elusive concept across to your students? We all look for those "Atta-Boys" or "Atta-Girls." In reality there are very few accolades out there for us because of our hard work. And to top it all, there are people out there who do a lot less work than we do, and they seem to be reaping the same benefits. So why work hard? Why put in the extra time and effort?

We are told that we should work hard for a very good reason:

> *Don't work hard only when your master is watching and then shirk when he isn't looking; work hard and with gladness all the time, as though working for Christ, doing the will of God with all of your hearts. Remember, the Lord will pay you for each good thing you do, whether you are slave or free*
>
> Ephesians 6: 6-8 (TLB)

We are told that we should gladly work hard all of the time because we are working for the Lord. He promises us rewards for each good thing we do. God tells us that if we serve, we should serve well, not to please others, but to please Him. We are to work hard because we serve God with all of our heart. Being noticed by our employers here on Earth is nice. It is gratifying to have someone recognize our hard work and professional attitudes. But our hearts and minds should belong to God. He is the one we are working to please.

So who benefits from our hard work? Our children do! They are rewarded many times over as a result of our efforts. The children reap what we sow. This is the entire purpose of the service spirit - others benefit from our work. Our benefits are our rewards in Heaven.

Dear Father,

Thank You for the eternal reward that You have given us, and thank You for giving us the service spirit. Help us to continue our service spirit to the benefit of Your children.

Amen

## YOUR SYMPHONY

If you have not seen the movie "Mr. Holland's Opus", I suggest that you see it right away. It is about a music teacher who begins his teaching career with an "8-4" attitude. He learns that teaching is more than imparting knowledge; it is also giving the children a "compass" so that they know how to use that knowledge. As the years go by, he realizes that his calling is to provide direction for each individual student. At the end of the movie, he finds himself in an auditorium surrounded by his past and present students. He is exalted for his dedication to his students and to his profession. He realizes that the symphony he has worked on for 30+ years is not only notes on paper, but also the lives of the students that he has touched.

Paul tells us the way to keep perfect harmony in our lives:

*Most of all, let love guide your life, for then the whole church will stay together in perfect harmony*
Colossians 3:14 (TLB)

Chances are you will not be able to gather all of your past and present students in one room at the end of your career. But if you could, what kind of symphony would they be playing about you? I hope it will be a symphony of love, adoration, respect, and appreciation. We know that there is more to education than most people realize. We are truly here to lead children, not just to impart knowledge. So have fun with your children and continue to show them the right path. Be their compass, and one day they will collectively be your symphony.

Dear Father,
    We realize that we are creating a symphony of lives as we mold Your children according to Your will. Help us to love all children so that they will sing Your praises.

Amen

CHAPTER 11

# JUNE/JULY

June is a month for reflections and farewells. We say goodbye to our students and to our colleagues for a while. We also reflect on our students' and our own accomplishments for the year. We wrap-up the school year in many ways: paper work (our writer's cramps will attest to that), evaluation of school goals, evaluation of personal goals, prepare our rooms for the Summer, begin planning for next year, etc. Along with the ending of another school year, Flag Day and Father's Day give us reasons to celebrate. Summer officially begins this month.

Summer is a time for self and family. No longer "on-call" and with no planning or grading during our off-hours, we can give our families and ourselves some much needed attention. We rest, relax, and rejuvenate as well as play hard during our Summer vacation.

Take time this summer to celebrate our profession. We are doing God's work as we raise His children in His will. God has placed us in the perfect position to change the future for many people. We are making our mark on this Earth by improving the quality of life for the next generation. We are making our mark in Heaven by adding more souls to spend eternity with God. I know God is pleased with us. Talk to Him and ask for His strength and guidance as we continue our efforts to serve His children.

## FINAL PRAYER

You are especially blessed because you have selflessly devoted your life to serving God's children. God is always with you. He will give you the strength and wisdom that you need to ensure that His children grow in His will. Call upon Him whenever you need His counsel or His comfort. He is waiting.

*The Lord bless you and keep you;*
*The Lord make His face shine upon you,*
*And be gracious to you;*
*The Lord lift up His countenance upon you,*
*And give you peace.*

Numbers 6:24-26 (NKJV)